50 Indonesian Snack Recipes for Home

By: Kelly Johnson

Table of Contents

- Lemper Ayam (Sticky Rice with Chicken)
- Pastel Goreng (Fried Savory Pastry)
- Pisang Goreng (Fried Banana Fritters)
- Martabak Manis (Indonesian Sweet Pancake)
- Tahu Goreng (Fried Tofu)
- Perkedel Kentang (Indonesian Potato Fritters)
- Klepon (Sweet Rice Cake Balls)
- Kue Cubit (Indonesian Pancake Bites)
- Kue Lapis Legit (Indonesian Layer Cake)
- Risoles (Indonesian Fried Spring Rolls)
- Bakwan Jagung (Indonesian Corn Fritters)
- Kue Lumpur (Indonesian Mud Cake)
- Dadar Gulung (Rolled Coconut Pancakes)
- Lumpia Goreng (Fried Spring Rolls)
- Kue Pukis (Indonesian Coconut Pancakes)
- Bolu Pisang (Banana Cake)
- Serabi (Indonesian Pancakes)
- Kue Lapis Surabaya (Surabaya Layer Cake)
- Kue Lumpur Singkong (Cassava Mud Cake)
- Klepon Ketan Hitam (Black Sticky Rice Cake Balls)
- Kue Lumpur Ketan (Sticky Rice Mud Cake)
- Bakwan Udang (Shrimp Fritters)
- Kue Lumpur Pisang (Banana Mud Cake)
- Kue Kering Nastar (Pineapple Tart Cookies)
- Kue Lumpur Coklat (Chocolate Mud Cake)
- Kue Lumpur Pandan (Pandan Mud Cake)
- Kue Lumpur Tape (Fermented Cassava Mud Cake)
- Kue Lumpur Keju (Cheese Mud Cake)
- Kue Lumpur Keju Coklat (Chocolate Cheese Mud Cake)
- Bolu Kukus (Steamed Sponge Cake)
- Kue Lumpur Ubi (Sweet Potato Mud Cake)
- Kue Lumpur Nangka (Jackfruit Mud Cake)
- Kue Lumpur Ubi Ungu (Purple Sweet Potato Mud Cake)
- Kue Lumpur Durian (Durian Mud Cake)
- Kue Lumpur Labu (Pumpkin Mud Cake)

- Kue Lumpur Pisang Keju (Banana Cheese Mud Cake)
- Kue Lumpur Nenas (Pineapple Mud Cake)
- Kue Lumpur Stroberi (Strawberry Mud Cake)
- Kue Lumpur Anggur (Grape Mud Cake)
- Kue Lumpur Mangga (Mango Mud Cake)
- Kue Lumpur Tiramisu (Tiramisu Mud Cake)
- Klepon Ketan (Sticky Rice Cake Balls)
- Kue Lapis Legit Prune (Prune Layer Cake)
- Kue Cubit Pandan (Pandan Pancake Bites)
- Kue Lumpur Keju Jagung (Cheese Corn Mud Cake)
- Risoles Sayur (Vegetable Spring Rolls)
- Dadar Gulung Pandan (Pandan Rolled Coconut Pancakes)
- Kue Lumpur Kacang (Peanut Mud Cake)
- Kue Lumpur Siap (Chicken Mud Cake)
- Bika Ambon (Indonesian Honeycomb Cake)

Lemper Ayam (Sticky Rice with Chicken)

Ingredients:

For the Sticky Rice:

- 2 cups glutinous rice (sticky rice), soaked in water for at least 3 hours or overnight
- 1 cup coconut milk
- 1 teaspoon salt

For the Chicken Filling:

- 2 boneless, skinless chicken breasts, diced into small pieces
- 2 cloves garlic, minced
- 1 shallot, minced
- 1 tablespoon cooking oil
- 2 tablespoons sweet soy sauce (kecap manis)
- 1 teaspoon ground coriander
- 1/2 teaspoon ground turmeric
- Salt and pepper, to taste
- Banana leaves, cut into rectangles and lightly heated over a flame to soften

Instructions:

Prepare the Sticky Rice:
- Drain the soaked glutinous rice and rinse it under cold water until the water runs clear.
- In a saucepan, combine the rinsed sticky rice, coconut milk, and salt. Cook over medium heat, stirring occasionally, until the rice absorbs the coconut milk and becomes sticky. Remove from heat and set aside.

Prepare the Chicken Filling:
- In a skillet, heat the cooking oil over medium heat. Add the minced garlic and shallot, and sauté until fragrant.
- Add the diced chicken breast to the skillet and cook until it is no longer pink.

- Stir in the sweet soy sauce, ground coriander, ground turmeric, salt, and pepper. Cook for another 2-3 minutes until the chicken is well coated and the flavors are combined. Remove from heat and let it cool slightly.

Assemble the Lemper Ayam:
- Take a piece of banana leaf and place a spoonful of sticky rice on it. Use the back of the spoon to flatten the rice into a thin layer.
- Spoon some of the cooked chicken filling onto the center of the rice.
- Fold the banana leaf over the filling to encase it, then fold in the sides to form a rectangular packet. Secure with toothpicks if needed.
- Repeat the process with the remaining sticky rice and chicken filling.

Steam the Lemper Ayam:
- Arrange the wrapped Lemper Ayam in a steamer basket, making sure to leave some space between each packet.
- Steam over boiling water for about 30-40 minutes, or until the sticky rice is fully cooked and the chicken filling is tender.
- Once cooked, remove the Lemper Ayam from the steamer and let them cool slightly before serving.

Serve the Lemper Ayam warm or at room temperature as a delicious snack or appetizer.

Enjoy your homemade Lemper Ayam, with its fragrant sticky rice and flavorful chicken filling wrapped in banana leaves!

Pastel Goreng (Fried Savory Pastry)

Ingredients:

For the Pastry Dough:

- 2 cups all-purpose flour
- 1/2 teaspoon salt
- 1/4 cup cold butter, diced
- 1/4 cup cold water

For the Filling:

- 2 tablespoons cooking oil
- 1 onion, finely chopped
- 2 cloves garlic, minced
- 200g ground chicken or beef
- 1 carrot, finely diced
- 1 potato, finely diced
- 1/2 cup green peas (fresh or frozen)
- 1 teaspoon curry powder
- Salt and pepper, to taste
- Water, as needed

For Frying:

- Cooking oil, for deep frying

Instructions:

Prepare the Pastry Dough:
- In a large mixing bowl, combine the all-purpose flour and salt. Add the cold diced butter.
- Use your fingertips to rub the butter into the flour until the mixture resembles coarse crumbs.

- Gradually add the cold water, a little at a time, and mix until a smooth dough forms. Wrap the dough in plastic wrap and refrigerate for at least 30 minutes.

Prepare the Filling:
- Heat cooking oil in a skillet over medium heat. Add the chopped onion and minced garlic, and sauté until fragrant.
- Add the ground chicken or beef to the skillet and cook until browned.
- Stir in the diced carrot, potato, and green peas. Cook for a few minutes until the vegetables are slightly softened.
- Add the curry powder, salt, and pepper to the skillet, and mix well. If the mixture is too dry, add a splash of water to moisten. Cook until the vegetables are tender and the filling is cooked through. Remove from heat and let it cool.

Assemble the Pastel Goreng:
- Divide the chilled pastry dough into small balls, about the size of a golf ball.
- Roll out each dough ball into a thin circle on a floured surface. Place a spoonful of the cooled filling in the center of each circle.
- Fold the dough over the filling to form a half-moon shape, then crimp the edges with a fork to seal.

Fry the Pastel Goreng:
- Heat cooking oil in a deep frying pan or pot over medium heat until hot.
- Carefully place the filled pastries in the hot oil, a few at a time, and fry until golden brown and crispy, turning occasionally.
- Once cooked, remove the pastries from the oil using a slotted spoon and drain on paper towels to remove excess oil.

Serve the Pastel Goreng hot as a delicious snack or appetizer.

Enjoy your homemade Pastel Goreng, with its crispy pastry shell and savory filling, perfect for any occasion!

Pisang Goreng (Fried Banana Fritters)

Ingredients:

- 4 ripe bananas (preferably Pisang Raja or other cooking bananas)
- 1 cup all-purpose flour
- 2 tablespoons rice flour (optional, for extra crispiness)
- 1/4 cup sugar (adjust to taste)
- 1/2 teaspoon baking powder
- 1/4 teaspoon salt
- 1/2 teaspoon vanilla extract (optional)
- 1/2 cup water (adjust as needed)
- Cooking oil, for frying

Instructions:

Peel the bananas and slice them into halves or quarters, depending on your preference. Set aside.

In a mixing bowl, combine the all-purpose flour, rice flour (if using), sugar, baking powder, and salt. Mix well to combine.

Gradually add water to the dry ingredients, stirring continuously, until you achieve a smooth batter consistency. Add more water if needed, but be careful not to make the batter too runny.

Heat cooking oil in a deep frying pan or pot over medium heat. The oil should be hot enough to fry the bananas but not smoking.

Dip each banana slice into the batter, ensuring it is fully coated.

Carefully place the coated banana slices into the hot oil, a few at a time, making sure not to overcrowd the pan.

Fry the banana slices until they are golden brown and crispy, turning them occasionally to ensure even cooking.

Once the banana fritters are cooked to perfection, remove them from the oil using a slotted spoon and transfer them to a plate lined with paper towels to drain excess oil.

Repeat the process with the remaining banana slices and batter until all the bananas are fried.

Serve the Pisang Goreng warm as a delightful snack or dessert. You can enjoy them on their own or with a sprinkle of powdered sugar or a drizzle of chocolate syrup for extra sweetness.

Enjoy the crispy, golden Pisang Goreng with your family and friends, savoring the irresistible combination of sweet bananas and crunchy coating!

This recipe yields deliciously crispy and golden Pisang Goreng that is sure to be a hit with everyone!

Martabak Manis (Indonesian Sweet Pancake)

Ingredients:

For the Batter:

- 2 cups all-purpose flour
- 1/2 teaspoon baking powder
- 1/4 teaspoon baking soda
- 1/4 teaspoon salt
- 2 tablespoons granulated sugar
- 1 large egg
- 1 1/2 cups coconut milk
- 1/2 cup water
- 1/2 teaspoon vanilla extract (optional)

For the Filling:

- Chocolate sprinkles or chocolate spread
- Grated cheese
- Crushed peanuts
- Sweetened condensed milk

For Topping:

- Butter or margarine, for greasing
- Powdered sugar, for dusting (optional)

Instructions:

In a large mixing bowl, whisk together the all-purpose flour, baking powder, baking soda, salt, and granulated sugar.
In a separate bowl, beat the egg lightly, then add coconut milk, water, and vanilla extract (if using). Mix until well combined.
Gradually pour the wet ingredients into the dry ingredients, stirring continuously until you get a smooth batter. Make sure there are no lumps in the batter.

Heat a non-stick skillet or griddle over medium heat. Grease the surface lightly with butter or margarine.

Pour a ladleful of batter onto the skillet, spreading it out into a thin circle with the back of the ladle.

Cook the pancake for about 2-3 minutes until bubbles form on the surface and the edges start to lift.

Sprinkle the desired filling evenly over the surface of the pancake. You can use chocolate sprinkles, grated cheese, crushed peanuts, or a combination of these fillings.

Carefully fold the pancake in half to enclose the filling, then cook for another 2-3 minutes until golden brown and crispy.

Transfer the Martabak Manis to a serving plate and drizzle with sweetened condensed milk. You can also sprinkle powdered sugar on top for extra sweetness.

Repeat the process with the remaining batter and fillings until all the pancakes are cooked.

Cut the Martabak Manis into slices and serve warm as a delicious snack or dessert.

Enjoy the indulgent and flavorful Martabak Manis with your family and friends, savoring the delightful combination of sweet fillings and fluffy pancakes!

Feel free to customize the fillings according to your preferences, and get creative with different combinations to make this sweet pancake truly your own.

Tahu Goreng (Fried Tofu)

Ingredients:

- 1 block of firm tofu
- 2 tablespoons cornstarch or all-purpose flour
- 1 teaspoon garlic powder (optional)
- 1/2 teaspoon salt, or to taste
- Vegetable oil, for frying

For the Sauce (optional):

- 2 tablespoons sweet soy sauce (kecap manis)
- 1 tablespoon soy sauce
- 1 teaspoon tamarind paste or vinegar
- 1 teaspoon sugar
- 1 clove garlic, minced
- 1 small red chili, thinly sliced (optional)
- Water, as needed

Instructions:

Press the tofu: Place the block of tofu between two paper towels and set something heavy on top, like a plate or a cutting board. Let it sit for about 15-20 minutes to press out excess moisture.

Cut the tofu: Once pressed, cut the tofu into cubes or rectangles, depending on your preference.

Prepare the coating: In a shallow dish, mix together the cornstarch or flour, garlic powder (if using), and salt.

Coat the tofu: Gently coat each tofu piece in the flour mixture, shaking off any excess.

Heat the oil: In a deep frying pan or pot, heat vegetable oil over medium-high heat until hot. You can test if the oil is ready by dropping a small piece of tofu into it; if it sizzles and bubbles, it's ready.

Fry the tofu: Carefully place the coated tofu pieces into the hot oil, making sure not to overcrowd the pan. Fry in batches if necessary. Cook the tofu for 2-3 minutes on each side, or until golden brown and crispy.

Drain the tofu: Once cooked, use a slotted spoon to transfer the fried tofu to a plate lined with paper towels to drain excess oil.

Make the sauce (optional): In a small saucepan, combine the sweet soy sauce, soy sauce, tamarind paste or vinegar, sugar, minced garlic, sliced chili (if using), and a splash of water. Cook over low heat, stirring occasionally, until the sauce is heated through and slightly thickened.

Serve: Serve the fried tofu hot, either on its own or with the prepared sauce drizzled on top. Enjoy as a snack, appetizer, or part of a larger meal.

Enjoy your homemade Tahu Goreng!

Feel free to customize the seasoning and sauce according to your taste preferences.

Tahu Goreng is versatile and can be enjoyed in various ways, so don't hesitate to get creative with your toppings and dipping sauces!

Perkedel Kentang (Indonesian Potato Fritters)

Ingredients:

- 500 grams potatoes (about 3-4 medium-sized potatoes)
- 1 small onion, finely chopped
- 2 cloves garlic, minced
- 2 green onions, finely chopped
- 1 teaspoon salt, or to taste
- 1/2 teaspoon ground white pepper
- 1/2 teaspoon ground coriander
- 1/4 teaspoon ground nutmeg
- 1 egg, beaten
- 2 tablespoons all-purpose flour (optional, for binding)
- Vegetable oil, for frying

Instructions:

Peel the potatoes and cut them into chunks. Place them in a pot of salted water and boil until tender, about 15-20 minutes.

Drain the potatoes and mash them while they're still warm until smooth and lump-free.

In a large mixing bowl, combine the mashed potatoes with the chopped onion, minced garlic, chopped green onions, salt, white pepper, ground coriander, and ground nutmeg. Mix well to incorporate all the ingredients.

Taste the mixture and adjust the seasoning if needed. You can add more salt or spices according to your preference.

If the mixture seems too wet, you can add a couple of tablespoons of all-purpose flour to help bind the ingredients together. Mix until well combined.

Shape the potato mixture into small patties or balls, depending on your preference. You can use your hands or a spoon to shape them.

Heat vegetable oil in a large frying pan or skillet over medium heat. The oil should be hot enough to fry the fritters but not smoking.

Once the oil is hot, carefully place the potato patties or balls into the pan, making sure not to overcrowd them. Fry in batches if necessary.

Cook the fritters for 3-4 minutes on each side, or until they are golden brown and crispy.

Once cooked, remove the fritters from the oil and transfer them to a plate lined with paper towels to drain excess oil.

Serve the Perkedel Kentang hot as a snack or side dish. They are delicious on their own or with a dipping sauce of your choice, such as chili sauce or sweet soy sauce.

Enjoy your homemade Perkedel Kentang!

Klepon (Sweet Rice Cake Balls)

Ingredients:

For the Filling:

- 100 grams palm sugar (gula jawa), cut into small cubes

For the Dough:

- 200 grams glutinous rice flour
- 1/4 teaspoon salt
- 150 ml warm water (approximately)
- Pandan leaves (optional, for aroma)

For Coating:

- 100 grams grated coconut
- A pinch of salt

Instructions:

Prepare the Filling:
- Take small portions of palm sugar and shape them into small cubes. Set aside.

Prepare the Dough:
- In a mixing bowl, combine the glutinous rice flour and salt. Gradually add warm water while stirring continuously until a smooth dough forms. The dough should be soft and pliable but not too sticky.
- If desired, add pandan leaves to the water while mixing to infuse the dough with pandan aroma.

Shape the Dough:
- Take a small portion of dough (about 1 tablespoon) and flatten it in your palm.
- Place a cube of palm sugar in the center of the dough.

- Carefully wrap the dough around the palm sugar to encase it completely. Roll it into a smooth ball between your palms. Ensure there are no cracks in the dough, or the palm sugar may leak out during cooking.
- Repeat the process with the remaining dough and palm sugar cubes.

Cook the Klepon:
- Bring a large pot of water to a gentle boil.
- Carefully drop the Klepon into the boiling water, ensuring they are not overcrowded. Cook them in batches if necessary.
- Boil the Klepon for about 2-3 minutes or until they float to the surface. Be careful not to overcook them, as they may become too soft.
- Once they float, remove the Klepon from the water using a slotted spoon and drain them briefly.

Coat the Klepon:
- In a shallow bowl, combine the grated coconut with a pinch of salt.
- Roll the cooked Klepon in the grated coconut until they are evenly coated.

Serve:
- Arrange the Klepon on a serving platter and serve them warm or at room temperature.
- Enjoy these delicious and aromatic Klepon as a delightful snack or dessert!

Klepon is best enjoyed fresh on the day they are made. If you have leftovers, store them in an airtight container at room temperature and consume within a day or two. Enjoy!

Kue Cubit (Indonesian Pancake Bites)

Ingredients:

- 1 cup all-purpose flour
- 1/4 cup granulated sugar
- 1 teaspoon baking powder
- 1/4 teaspoon baking soda
- 1/4 teaspoon salt
- 1 egg
- 3/4 cup milk
- 2 tablespoons melted butter or vegetable oil
- 1 teaspoon vanilla extract
- Toppings of your choice (chocolate chips, sprinkles, cheese, etc.)
- Vegetable oil or butter for greasing the pan

Instructions:

In a mixing bowl, combine the all-purpose flour, sugar, baking powder, baking soda, and salt. Mix well to combine.

In a separate bowl, whisk together the egg, milk, melted butter or vegetable oil, and vanilla extract until well combined.

Pour the wet ingredients into the dry ingredients and stir until just combined. Be careful not to overmix; a few lumps in the batter are okay.

Heat a non-stick pan or griddle over medium heat. Lightly grease the pan with vegetable oil or butter.

Spoon about 1 tablespoon of batter onto the hot pan for each pancake bite. Leave some space between each pancake as they will spread slightly.

Once small bubbles form on the surface of the pancake and the edges start to set, sprinkle your desired toppings (chocolate chips, sprinkles, cheese, etc.) onto each pancake.

Using a spatula, carefully flip each pancake and cook for another 1-2 minutes, or until golden brown on the bottom and cooked through.

Remove the pancake bites from the pan and repeat the process with the remaining batter.

Serve the Kue Cubit warm as a delightful snack or dessert. You can enjoy them plain or drizzle them with chocolate syrup or condensed milk for extra sweetness.

Enjoy your homemade Kue Cubit with family and friends, savoring the fluffy texture and delicious toppings!

Feel free to get creative with the toppings and flavorings to suit your taste preferences. Kue Cubit is a versatile treat that can be customized in many ways, making it perfect for any occasion.

Kue Lapis Legit (Indonesian Layer Cake)

Ingredients:

- 500 grams unsalted butter, softened
- 250 grams granulated sugar
- 12 large eggs, separated
- 200 grams all-purpose flour
- 100 grams cornstarch
- 1 teaspoon ground cinnamon
- 1/2 teaspoon ground nutmeg
- 1/4 teaspoon ground cloves
- 1/4 teaspoon salt
- 1 teaspoon vanilla extract
- 1/2 teaspoon almond extract (optional)
- Butter or vegetable oil, for greasing the pan

Instructions:

Preheat your oven to 160°C (320°F). Grease a 20x20 cm (8x8 inch) square baking pan with butter or vegetable oil and line the bottom with parchment paper. Set aside.
In a large mixing bowl, cream together the softened butter and granulated sugar until light and fluffy.
Add the egg yolks one at a time, mixing well after each addition.
In a separate bowl, sift together the all-purpose flour, cornstarch, ground cinnamon, ground nutmeg, ground cloves, and salt.
Gradually add the dry ingredients to the butter mixture, mixing until well combined.
In another clean mixing bowl, beat the egg whites until stiff peaks form.
Gently fold the beaten egg whites into the cake batter until just combined. Be careful not to overmix.
Divide the batter into two equal portions. Add the vanilla extract to one portion and the almond extract (if using) to the other portion, mixing until well combined.
Pour a thin layer of the vanilla-flavored batter into the prepared baking pan and spread it evenly with a spatula. Bake in the preheated oven for about 10-12 minutes, or until the layer is set and lightly golden on top.

Once the first layer is baked, remove the pan from the oven and carefully pour a thin layer of the almond-flavored batter on top of the baked layer. Return the pan to the oven and bake for another 10-12 minutes, or until set and lightly golden. Continue alternating between the vanilla and almond-flavored batters, baking each layer until the cake is about 20-25 layers high and golden brown on top. Once all layers are baked, remove the cake from the oven and let it cool completely in the pan.

Once cooled, carefully remove the cake from the pan and trim the edges if necessary. Slice the cake into squares or rectangles and serve.

Enjoy your homemade Kue Lapis Legit as a delightful treat with a cup of tea or coffee!

Note: Kue Lapis Legit can be stored in an airtight container at room temperature for up to one week or refrigerated for longer shelf life. Allow it to come to room temperature before serving for the best taste and texture.

Risoles (Indonesian Fried Spring Rolls)

Ingredients:

For the Filling:

- 200 grams chicken breast, cooked and shredded (or use ground meat of your choice)
- 1 medium carrot, finely diced
- 1 small onion, finely chopped
- 2 cloves garlic, minced
- 1/2 cup frozen peas
- 1/4 cup diced cooked potatoes (optional)
- 1 tablespoon cooking oil
- Salt and pepper to taste
- 1/2 teaspoon ground nutmeg (optional)
- 1/2 teaspoon ground white pepper
- 1 tablespoon soy sauce
- 1 tablespoon oyster sauce
- 1 tablespoon sweet soy sauce (kecap manis)
- 1 tablespoon cornstarch or all-purpose flour
- 1 cup chicken or vegetable broth
- Grated cheese (optional)

For the Wrappers:

- Spring roll wrappers (you can find them in Asian grocery stores)

For Frying:

- Vegetable oil for frying

For Coating:

- 2 eggs, beaten
- Breadcrumbs

Instructions:

Prepare the Filling:

- Heat cooking oil in a pan over medium heat. Add the chopped onions and minced garlic and sauté until fragrant.
- Add the diced carrots and cook for a few minutes until they start to soften.
- Add the shredded chicken (or ground meat) to the pan and cook until it's no longer pink.
- Stir in the frozen peas and cooked potatoes (if using), then season with salt, pepper, ground nutmeg (if using), and ground white pepper.
- Add soy sauce, oyster sauce, and sweet soy sauce to the filling mixture. Mix well.
- In a small bowl, mix cornstarch or all-purpose flour with chicken or vegetable broth until smooth. Pour this mixture into the filling and stir until it thickens. Cook for another minute or until the filling is well combined and has thickened. Remove from heat and let it cool.
- Optionally, mix in grated cheese to the cooled filling for extra flavor.

Assemble the Risoles:
- Take a spring roll wrapper and place it on a clean surface with one corner pointing towards you.
- Spoon a small amount of the filling onto the wrapper, spreading it in a line across the bottom edge of the wrapper.
- Fold the bottom corner of the wrapper over the filling, then fold the sides towards the center, and roll it up tightly into a cylinder. Seal the edge with a little water or beaten egg.
- Repeat the process with the remaining wrappers and filling.

Coat and Fry the Risoles:
- Dip each rolled risole into the beaten egg, then coat it with breadcrumbs, ensuring it's evenly coated.
- Heat vegetable oil in a deep frying pan or pot over medium heat.
- Once the oil is hot, carefully add the risoles in batches and fry until golden brown and crispy, turning occasionally for even cooking.
- Remove the fried risoles from the oil using a slotted spoon and drain on paper towels to remove excess oil.

Serve:
- Serve the crispy Risoles hot with your favorite dipping sauce, such as chili sauce or sweet chili sauce.
- Enjoy your homemade Indonesian Fried Spring Rolls as a delightful snack or appetizer!

Note: You can also bake the risoles in the oven if you prefer a healthier option. Preheat the oven to 200°C (400°F) and place the coated risoles on a baking sheet lined with parchment paper. Bake for about 15-20 minutes, turning halfway through, until they are golden brown and crispy.

Bakwan Jagung (Indonesian Corn Fritters)

Ingredients:

- 2 cups fresh corn kernels (from about 2-3 ears of corn) or canned corn, drained
- 1 cup all-purpose flour
- 2 tablespoons rice flour or cornstarch (optional, for extra crispiness)
- 1/2 cup chopped green onions
- 1/4 cup chopped celery leaves
- 1-2 red chilies, finely chopped (optional, adjust to taste)
- 2 cloves garlic, minced
- 1 teaspoon ground coriander
- 1/2 teaspoon ground turmeric
- 1/2 teaspoon ground cumin
- 1/2 teaspoon salt, or to taste
- 1/4 teaspoon ground black pepper
- 1 egg, lightly beaten
- 1/2 cup water (adjust as needed)
- Vegetable oil, for frying

Instructions:

In a large mixing bowl, combine the fresh corn kernels (or canned corn), all-purpose flour, rice flour or cornstarch (if using), chopped green onions, chopped celery leaves, chopped red chilies (if using), minced garlic, ground coriander, ground turmeric, ground cumin, salt, and black pepper. Mix well to combine.

Add the lightly beaten egg to the bowl and mix until all ingredients are evenly coated with the egg.

Gradually add water to the mixture, stirring continuously, until you achieve a thick batter consistency. The batter should coat the back of a spoon but still be pourable.

Heat vegetable oil in a deep frying pan or pot over medium heat. The oil should be hot enough to fry the fritters but not smoking.

Once the oil is hot, carefully drop spoonfuls of the batter into the hot oil, making sure not to overcrowd the pan. You can use a spoon or your hands to shape the fritters.

Fry the fritters in batches, turning occasionally, until they are golden brown and crispy on all sides, about 3-4 minutes per batch.

Once cooked, remove the fritters from the oil using a slotted spoon and transfer them to a plate lined with paper towels to drain excess oil.

Serve the Bakwan Jagung hot as a delicious snack or appetizer. You can enjoy them on their own or with a dipping sauce of your choice, such as chili sauce or sweet chili sauce.

Enjoy your homemade Indonesian Corn Fritters with family and friends, savoring the crispy exterior and flavorful interior!

Feel free to adjust the spiciness level by adding more or fewer red chilies according to your taste preferences. You can also customize the batter by adding other vegetables or herbs of your choice.

Kue Lumpur (Indonesian Mud Cake)

Ingredients:

- 200 grams glutinous rice flour
- 100 grams all-purpose flour
- 100 grams granulated sugar
- 1/4 teaspoon salt
- 2 tablespoons cocoa powder
- 1 teaspoon baking powder
- 200 ml coconut milk
- 100 ml water
- 2 eggs, beaten
- 2 tablespoons melted butter or margarine
- 1/2 teaspoon vanilla extract

For the Topping (optional):

- Powdered sugar for dusting
- Grated cheese
- Chocolate syrup or melted chocolate

Instructions:

Preheat your oven to 180°C (350°F). Grease a baking dish or cake pan with butter or cooking spray and set aside.

In a large mixing bowl, sift together the glutinous rice flour, all-purpose flour, cocoa powder, baking powder, granulated sugar, and salt. Mix well to combine.

In a separate bowl, mix together the beaten eggs, coconut milk, water, melted butter or margarine, and vanilla extract until well combined.

Gradually pour the wet ingredients into the dry ingredients, stirring continuously until you get a smooth batter. Make sure there are no lumps in the batter.

Pour the batter into the greased baking dish or cake pan, spreading it out evenly.

Bake in the preheated oven for about 30-40 minutes, or until the top is set and a toothpick inserted into the center comes out clean. The texture of Kue Lumpur should be moist and slightly gooey in the center, resembling a pudding.

Once baked, remove the Kue Lumpur from the oven and let it cool slightly in the pan.

If desired, sprinkle powdered sugar over the top of the Kue Lumpur for a decorative touch. You can also drizzle melted chocolate or chocolate syrup over the top, or sprinkle grated cheese for extra flavor.

Slice the Kue Lumpur into squares or rectangles and serve warm as a delightful dessert. Enjoy with a cup of coffee or tea for the perfect indulgence!

Store any leftover Kue Lumpur in an airtight container at room temperature for up to 2-3 days. Reheat in the microwave for a few seconds before serving to enjoy it warm and gooey again.

Enjoy your homemade Indonesian Mud Cake and savor the rich, decadent flavors!

Dadar Gulung (Rolled Coconut Pancakes)

Ingredients:

For the Pandan Crepes:

- 1 cup all-purpose flour
- 1 cup coconut milk
- 1/2 cup water
- 2 eggs
- 1/4 teaspoon salt
- 1 tablespoon pandan extract or pandan paste (for flavor and green color)
- Vegetable oil or butter, for cooking

For the Sweet Coconut Filling:

- 200 grams grated coconut (fresh or frozen)
- 100 grams palm sugar or brown sugar, grated
- 1 pandan leaf, tied into a knot (optional, for added flavor)

Instructions:

Prepare the Sweet Coconut Filling:
- In a pan, combine the grated coconut, grated palm sugar or brown sugar, and pandan leaf (if using).
- Cook the mixture over medium heat, stirring continuously, until the sugar has melted and the coconut is evenly coated. Cook for about 5-7 minutes, or until the mixture is slightly sticky. Remove from heat and set aside to cool.

Make the Pandan Crepes:
- In a mixing bowl, whisk together the all-purpose flour, coconut milk, water, eggs, salt, and pandan extract or pandan paste until smooth and well combined. The batter should be thin and pourable.
- Heat a non-stick frying pan or crepe pan over medium heat. Lightly grease the pan with vegetable oil or butter.

- Pour a small ladleful of the batter into the center of the pan, swirling it around to spread the batter evenly and thinly across the bottom of the pan.
- Cook the crepe for about 1-2 minutes, or until the edges start to lift and the bottom is lightly golden. Flip the crepe and cook for another 1-2 minutes on the other side.
- Remove the cooked crepe from the pan and transfer it to a plate. Repeat the process with the remaining batter, stacking the cooked crepes on top of each other.

Assemble the Dadar Gulung:
- Take one cooked crepe and place it on a clean surface.
- Spoon a small amount of the sweet coconut filling onto one end of the crepe, then fold the sides over the filling and roll it up tightly into a cylinder. Repeat the process with the remaining crepes and filling.

Serve:
- Slice the rolled Dadar Gulung into smaller pieces, if desired, and serve them as a delightful snack or dessert.
- Optionally, you can sprinkle some grated coconut or powdered sugar on top of the rolled pancakes for extra flavor and presentation.

Enjoy your homemade Dadar Gulung with family and friends, savoring the delicious combination of pandan-flavored crepes and sweet coconut filling!

Note: You can adjust the sweetness of the coconut filling according to your taste preferences by adding more or less sugar. If you can't find pandan extract or pandan paste, you can substitute with vanilla extract or omit it altogether for plain crepes.

Lumpia Goreng (Fried Spring Rolls)

Ingredients:

For the Filling:

- 200 grams ground pork or chicken (or use shrimp or a combination of meats)
- 1 cup shredded cabbage
- 1 medium carrot, julienned or grated
- 1 small onion, finely chopped
- 2 cloves garlic, minced
- 1 tablespoon soy sauce
- 1 teaspoon fish sauce (optional)
- 1 teaspoon sugar
- 1/2 teaspoon ground black pepper
- 1 tablespoon vegetable oil
- Spring roll wrappers (about 20-25 pieces)
- Vegetable oil for frying

For Dipping Sauce (Optional):

- Sweet chili sauce
- Soy sauce
- Vinegar
- Minced garlic
- Sugar (optional)
- Chili flakes (optional)

Instructions:

Prepare the Filling:
- Heat vegetable oil in a pan over medium heat. Add the chopped onions and minced garlic, and sauté until fragrant.
- Add the ground pork or chicken to the pan and cook until browned and no longer pink.
- Stir in the shredded cabbage and julienned carrots, and cook for a few minutes until the vegetables are slightly softened.

- Season the filling with soy sauce, fish sauce (if using), sugar, and ground black pepper. Mix well to combine.
- Cook the filling for another 2-3 minutes, or until the vegetables are cooked through but still slightly crisp. Remove from heat and let it cool.

Assemble the Spring Rolls:
- Place a spring roll wrapper on a clean surface with one corner pointing towards you (keep the remaining wrappers covered with a damp towel to prevent them from drying out).
- Spoon about 1-2 tablespoons of the filling onto the bottom third of the wrapper.
- Fold the bottom corner of the wrapper over the filling, then fold the sides towards the center, and roll it up tightly into a cylinder. Seal the edge with a little water.
- Repeat the process with the remaining wrappers and filling.

Fry the Spring Rolls:
- Heat vegetable oil in a deep frying pan or pot over medium-high heat. The oil should be hot enough to fry the spring rolls but not smoking.
- Once the oil is hot, carefully add the spring rolls in batches, making sure not to overcrowd the pan.
- Fry the spring rolls for about 3-4 minutes per batch, or until they are golden brown and crispy on all sides.
- Once cooked, remove the spring rolls from the oil using a slotted spoon and transfer them to a plate lined with paper towels to drain excess oil.

Serve:
- Serve the Lumpia Goreng hot as a delicious appetizer or snack.
- Optionally, serve with a dipping sauce made with sweet chili sauce mixed with soy sauce, vinegar, minced garlic, sugar (optional), and chili flakes (optional).

Enjoy your homemade Fried Spring Rolls with family and friends, savoring the crispy exterior and savory filling!

Note: You can customize the filling by adding other vegetables or ingredients of your choice, such as bean sprouts, bamboo shoots, mushrooms, or tofu. Adjust the seasoning according to your taste preferences.

Kue Pukis (Indonesian Coconut Pancakes)

Ingredients:

- 200 grams all-purpose flour
- 100 grams rice flour
- 100 grams granulated sugar
- 1/2 teaspoon salt
- 1 teaspoon baking powder
- 200 ml coconut milk
- 200 ml water
- 2 eggs
- 1 teaspoon vanilla extract
- Butter or cooking oil, for greasing the mold

Optional Toppings:

- Grated coconut
- Chocolate sprinkles
- Condensed milk
- Jam or jelly

Special Equipment:

- Kue Pukis mold (available at Asian grocery stores or online)

Instructions:

In a large mixing bowl, combine the all-purpose flour, rice flour, granulated sugar, salt, and baking powder. Mix well to combine.
In a separate bowl, whisk together the coconut milk, water, eggs, and vanilla extract until well combined.
Gradually pour the wet ingredients into the dry ingredients, stirring continuously, until you get a smooth batter. The batter should be thin and pourable.
Preheat your Kue Pukis mold over medium heat. Once the mold is hot, lightly grease each indentation with butter or cooking oil.

Pour the batter into each indentation of the mold, filling them about three-quarters full.

Close the lid of the mold and cook the Kue Pukis for about 2-3 minutes, or until the bottom is golden brown and the top is set.

Carefully open the lid and flip each Kue Pukis using a skewer or fork. Cook for another 1-2 minutes, or until the other side is golden brown and cooked through.

Once cooked, remove the Kue Pukis from the mold and transfer them to a plate.

Repeat the process with the remaining batter, greasing the mold as needed.

Serve the Kue Pukis warm with your choice of toppings, such as grated coconut, chocolate sprinkles, condensed milk, or jam.

Enjoy your homemade Indonesian Coconut Pancakes as a delightful snack or dessert, savoring the sweet and coconutty flavor!

Note: You can adjust the sweetness of the Kue Pukis batter by adding more or less sugar according to your taste preferences. Experiment with different toppings to create your favorite flavor combinations.

Bolu Pisang (Banana Cake)

Ingredients:

- 3 ripe bananas, mashed
- 1 1/2 cups all-purpose flour
- 1 teaspoon baking powder
- 1/2 teaspoon baking soda
- 1/4 teaspoon salt
- 1/2 cup unsalted butter, softened
- 3/4 cup granulated sugar
- 2 eggs
- 1 teaspoon vanilla extract
- 1/4 cup milk
- Optional: chopped nuts or chocolate chips for added texture and flavor

Instructions:

Preheat your oven to 350°F (175°C). Grease and flour a 9x5-inch loaf pan, or line it with parchment paper for easy removal.
In a medium bowl, sift together the all-purpose flour, baking powder, baking soda, and salt. Set aside.
In a large mixing bowl, cream together the softened butter and granulated sugar until light and fluffy.
Add the eggs, one at a time, to the butter-sugar mixture, beating well after each addition. Then, stir in the mashed bananas and vanilla extract until well combined.
Gradually add the dry ingredients to the wet ingredients, alternating with the milk, and mix until just combined. Be careful not to overmix.
If desired, fold in chopped nuts or chocolate chips into the batter for added flavor and texture.
Pour the batter into the prepared loaf pan and spread it evenly.
Bake in the preheated oven for 50-60 minutes, or until a toothpick inserted into the center of the cake comes out clean.
Once baked, remove the cake from the oven and let it cool in the pan for about 10 minutes before transferring it to a wire rack to cool completely.
Once cooled, slice the Bolu Pisang into thick slices and serve. Enjoy the moist and delicious banana cake with a cup of tea or coffee!

Store any leftover cake in an airtight container at room temperature for up to 3 days, or in the refrigerator for longer freshness.

Feel free to customize your Bolu Pisang by adding your favorite mix-ins, such as chopped nuts, chocolate chips, or even shredded coconut. This versatile cake is perfect for breakfast, dessert, or as a sweet snack any time of the day.

Serabi (Indonesian Pancakes)

Ingredients:

For the Pancake Batter:

- 1 cup rice flour
- 1/4 cup all-purpose flour
- 1/2 teaspoon baking powder
- 1/4 teaspoon salt
- 1 cup coconut milk
- 1/4 cup water
- 2 tablespoons granulated sugar
- 1/2 teaspoon vanilla extract

For Toppings (Optional):

- Coconut syrup (gula jawa)
- Chocolate sauce
- Grated coconut
- Sliced bananas
- Sweetened condensed milk

Instructions:

In a mixing bowl, sift together the rice flour, all-purpose flour, baking powder, and salt. Mix well to combine.

In a separate bowl, whisk together the coconut milk, water, granulated sugar, and vanilla extract until the sugar is dissolved.

Gradually pour the wet ingredients into the dry ingredients, stirring continuously, until you get a smooth batter. The batter should be thin and pourable.

Heat a non-stick frying pan or griddle over medium heat. Lightly grease the pan with cooking spray or a little oil.

Pour a small ladleful of the pancake batter onto the hot pan, spreading it out evenly to form a thin pancake. You can make small pancakes (about 4 inches in diameter) or larger ones, depending on your preference.

Cook the pancake for about 2-3 minutes, or until bubbles form on the surface and the edges start to lift. Flip the pancake and cook for another 1-2 minutes on the other side, or until golden brown and cooked through.

Once cooked, remove the pancake from the pan and transfer it to a plate. Repeat the process with the remaining batter, greasing the pan as needed.

Serve the Serabi warm with your choice of toppings. Traditional toppings include coconut syrup (gula jawa), chocolate sauce, grated coconut, sliced bananas, or sweetened condensed milk.

Enjoy your homemade Indonesian Pancakes as a delightful snack or dessert, savoring the light and fluffy texture and delicious coconut flavor!

Note: You can adjust the sweetness of the pancake batter by adding more or less sugar according to your taste preferences. Feel free to get creative with the toppings and experiment with different flavors to create your favorite combinations.

Kue Lapis Surabaya (Surabaya Layer Cake)

Ingredients:

For the Cake Layers:

- 250 grams unsalted butter, softened
- 200 grams granulated sugar
- 6 eggs, separated
- 200 grams all-purpose flour
- 50 grams cornstarch
- 1/2 teaspoon baking powder
- 1/4 teaspoon salt
- 1 teaspoon vanilla extract
- 1/2 teaspoon ground cinnamon
- 1/4 teaspoon ground nutmeg
- 1/4 teaspoon ground cloves
- Yellow food coloring (optional)

For the Jam Filling:

- 300 grams fruit jam or preserves (traditionally pineapple jam is used)
- 2 tablespoons water
- 1 tablespoon lemon juice

Instructions:

Preheat your oven to 160°C (320°F). Grease and line two 20cm (8-inch) round cake pans with parchment paper.
In a large mixing bowl, cream together the softened butter and granulated sugar until light and fluffy.
Add the egg yolks to the butter-sugar mixture, one at a time, mixing well after each addition. Add the vanilla extract and mix until combined.
In a separate bowl, sift together the all-purpose flour, cornstarch, baking powder, salt, ground cinnamon, ground nutmeg, and ground cloves.
Gradually add the dry ingredients to the butter mixture, mixing until well combined. Set aside.

In another clean mixing bowl, beat the egg whites until stiff peaks form.
Gently fold the beaten egg whites into the cake batter until just combined. Be careful not to overmix.
If desired, divide the batter into two portions and add yellow food coloring to one portion to achieve a golden color for one layer of the cake.
Pour the batter into the prepared cake pans, spreading it out evenly.
Bake in the preheated oven for about 20-25 minutes, or until the cakes are lightly golden and spring back when lightly touched.
Once baked, remove the cakes from the oven and let them cool in the pans for about 10 minutes before transferring them to a wire rack to cool completely.
While the cakes are cooling, prepare the jam filling. In a small saucepan, heat the fruit jam or preserves with water and lemon juice over low heat, stirring occasionally, until it becomes slightly runny. Remove from heat and let it cool slightly.
Once the cakes and jam filling are cooled, assemble the Kue Lapis Surabaya.
Place one cake layer on a serving plate or cake stand. Spread a thin layer of jam filling evenly over the top.
Place the second cake layer on top of the jam filling. Repeat the process with the remaining jam filling, spreading it evenly over the top of the second cake layer.
Optionally, decorate the top of the cake with additional jam filling or powdered sugar for garnish.
Slice and serve the Kue Lapis Surabaya at room temperature, and enjoy the rich and flavorful layers of this traditional Indonesian delicacy!
Store any leftover cake in an airtight container at room temperature for up to 2-3 days, or in the refrigerator for longer shelf life. Bring it to room temperature before serving for the best taste and texture.

Kue Lumpur Singkong (Cassava Mud Cake)

Ingredients:

- 500 grams grated cassava (fresh or frozen, thawed)
- 200 ml coconut milk
- 150 grams palm sugar (gula jawa), grated or chopped
- 1/4 teaspoon salt
- Banana leaves or parchment paper, for lining the baking pan

Instructions:

Preheat your oven to 180°C (350°F). Grease a baking dish or cake pan with butter or cooking spray, and line it with banana leaves or parchment paper for easy removal.

In a mixing bowl, combine the grated cassava, coconut milk, palm sugar, and salt. Mix well until the ingredients are evenly incorporated.

Pour the cassava mixture into the prepared baking dish, spreading it out evenly.

Bake in the preheated oven for about 45-60 minutes, or until the top is set and golden brown, and a toothpick inserted into the center comes out clean.

Once baked, remove the Kue Lumpur Singkong from the oven and let it cool in the pan for about 10-15 minutes.

Once cooled slightly, carefully invert the Kue Lumpur Singkong onto a serving plate and remove the banana leaves or parchment paper.

Allow the cake to cool completely before slicing and serving.

Slice the Kue Lumpur Singkong into squares or rectangles, and serve it as a delicious dessert or snack.

Enjoy the rich and caramel-flavored Cassava Mud Cake with family and friends, savoring its unique texture and taste!

Store any leftover cake in an airtight container in the refrigerator for up to 3-4 days. You can reheat it in the microwave for a few seconds before serving to enjoy it warm.

Feel free to garnish the Kue Lumpur Singkong with grated coconut or a drizzle of palm sugar syrup for extra flavor and presentation.

Klepon Ketan Hitam (Black Sticky Rice Cake Balls)

Ingredients:

For the Filling:

- 100 grams palm sugar (gula jawa), chopped into small cubes
- Water for boiling

For the Dough:

- 200 grams glutinous black rice flour (ketan hitam)
- 50 grams glutinous rice flour
- 150 ml water
- 1/4 teaspoon salt

For Coating:

- 100 grams grated coconut
- A pinch of salt

Instructions:

Prepare the Filling:
- In a small saucepan, bring water to a boil. Add the chopped palm sugar and simmer until the sugar is completely dissolved. Remove from heat and let it cool slightly.

Make the Dough:
- In a mixing bowl, combine the glutinous black rice flour, glutinous rice flour, and salt. Gradually add water while kneading until a smooth and pliable dough is formed. The dough should be soft but not sticky.

Assemble the Klepon:
- Pinch off a small piece of dough and flatten it in your palm. Place a cube of palm sugar in the center and gently enclose it with the dough, shaping it into a small ball. Make sure the palm sugar is completely covered with dough to prevent it from leaking during cooking. Repeat this process with the remaining dough and palm sugar.

- Cook the Klepon:
    - Bring a pot of water to a boil. Carefully drop the Klepon into the boiling water and cook until they float to the surface, about 2-3 minutes. Once they float, let them cook for an additional 1-2 minutes to ensure they are cooked through.
- Prepare the Coating:
    - In a separate bowl, combine the grated coconut with a pinch of salt.
- Coat the Klepon:
    - Remove the cooked Klepon from the boiling water using a slotted spoon and immediately roll them in the grated coconut mixture until they are evenly coated.
- Serve:
    - Arrange the Klepon on a serving plate and serve them warm or at room temperature as a delicious snack or dessert.
- Enjoy your homemade Klepon Ketan Hitam, savoring the sweet and chewy texture and the rich flavor of palm sugar!
- Store any leftover Klepon in an airtight container at room temperature for up to 2-3 days. You can reheat them in the microwave for a few seconds before serving if desired.

Feel free to adjust the amount of palm sugar according to your preference for sweetness. You can also experiment with different fillings such as grated coconut or mashed sweet potatoes for variety.

Kue Lumpur Ketan (Sticky Rice Mud Cake)

Ingredients:

- 250 grams glutinous rice flour (ketan)
- 200 ml coconut milk
- 150 grams palm sugar (gula jawa), grated or chopped
- 1/4 teaspoon salt
- Banana leaves or parchment paper, for lining the baking pan

Instructions:

Preheat your oven to 180°C (350°F). Grease a baking dish or cake pan with butter or cooking spray, and line it with banana leaves or parchment paper for easy removal.

In a mixing bowl, combine the glutinous rice flour, coconut milk, palm sugar, and salt. Mix well until the ingredients are evenly incorporated.

Pour the mixture into the prepared baking dish, spreading it out evenly.

Bake in the preheated oven for about 45-60 minutes, or until the top is set and golden brown, and a toothpick inserted into the center comes out clean.

Once baked, remove the Kue Lumpur Ketan from the oven and let it cool in the pan for about 10-15 minutes.

Once cooled slightly, carefully invert the Kue Lumpur Ketan onto a serving plate and remove the banana leaves or parchment paper.

Allow the cake to cool completely before slicing and serving.

Slice the Kue Lumpur Ketan into squares or rectangles, and serve it as a delicious dessert or snack.

Enjoy the rich and caramel-flavored Sticky Rice Mud Cake with family and friends, savoring its unique texture and taste!

Store any leftover cake in an airtight container in the refrigerator for up to 3-4 days. You can reheat it in the microwave for a few seconds before serving to enjoy it warm.

Feel free to garnish the Kue Lumpur Ketan with grated coconut or a drizzle of palm sugar syrup for extra flavor and presentation.

Bakwan Udang (Shrimp Fritters)

Ingredients:

- 200 grams shrimp, peeled and deveined
- 1 carrot, grated
- 1 small onion, finely chopped
- 2-3 spring onions, finely chopped
- 1/2 cup cabbage, finely shredded
- 1/2 cup all-purpose flour
- 2 tablespoons cornstarch
- 1 teaspoon baking powder
- 1 teaspoon salt, or to taste
- 1/2 teaspoon ground white pepper
- 1/2 teaspoon garlic powder
- 1/2 teaspoon ground coriander (optional)
- 1/2 teaspoon ground cumin (optional)
- 1/4 teaspoon turmeric powder (optional)
- 1 egg
- 1/4 cup water
- Vegetable oil, for deep frying

Instructions:

In a food processor, pulse the shrimp until coarsely chopped. Alternatively, finely chop the shrimp using a knife.
In a large mixing bowl, combine the chopped shrimp, grated carrot, chopped onion, spring onions, and shredded cabbage.
In a separate bowl, sift together the all-purpose flour, cornstarch, baking powder, salt, ground white pepper, garlic powder, and any optional spices (ground coriander, ground cumin, and turmeric powder).
Add the dry ingredients to the shrimp and vegetable mixture. Mix well to combine.
In another small bowl, whisk together the egg and water. Pour the egg mixture into the batter and stir until everything is well coated and combined. The batter should have a thick consistency.
Heat vegetable oil in a deep fryer or large frying pan over medium heat. The oil should be hot enough to fry the fritters but not smoking.

Drop spoonfuls of the batter into the hot oil, making sure not to overcrowd the pan. Use a spoon to shape the batter into small fritters.

Fry the fritters for 3-4 minutes on each side, or until they are golden brown and crispy.

Once cooked, remove the fritters from the oil using a slotted spoon and transfer them to a plate lined with paper towels to drain excess oil.

Serve the Bakwan Udang hot with your favorite dipping sauce, such as sweet chili sauce or soy sauce with chopped chili and lime juice.

Enjoy your homemade Shrimp Fritters as a delicious snack or appetizer, savoring the crunchy exterior and flavorful shrimp and vegetable filling!

Store any leftover fritters in an airtight container in the refrigerator and reheat them in the oven or microwave before serving.

Kue Lumpur Pisang (Banana Mud Cake)

Ingredients:

- 3 ripe bananas, mashed
- 200 grams all-purpose flour
- 100 grams glutinous rice flour
- 200 ml coconut milk
- 150 grams palm sugar (gula jawa), grated or chopped
- 1/4 teaspoon salt
- 1/2 teaspoon baking powder
- 1/2 teaspoon vanilla extract
- Banana leaves or parchment paper, for lining the baking pan

Instructions:

Preheat your oven to 180°C (350°F). Grease a baking dish or cake pan with butter or cooking spray, and line it with banana leaves or parchment paper for easy removal.

In a mixing bowl, combine the mashed bananas, all-purpose flour, glutinous rice flour, coconut milk, palm sugar, salt, baking powder, and vanilla extract. Mix well until the ingredients are evenly incorporated and the batter is smooth.

Pour the batter into the prepared baking dish, spreading it out evenly.

Bake in the preheated oven for about 45-60 minutes, or until the top is set and golden brown, and a toothpick inserted into the center comes out clean.

Once baked, remove the Kue Lumpur Pisang from the oven and let it cool in the pan for about 10-15 minutes.

Once cooled slightly, carefully invert the Kue Lumpur Pisang onto a serving plate and remove the banana leaves or parchment paper.

Allow the cake to cool completely before slicing and serving.

Slice the Kue Lumpur Pisang into squares or rectangles, and serve it as a delicious dessert or snack.

Enjoy the rich and caramel-flavored Banana Mud Cake with family and friends, savoring its unique texture and taste!

Store any leftover cake in an airtight container in the refrigerator for up to 3-4 days. You can reheat it in the microwave for a few seconds before serving to enjoy it warm.

Feel free to garnish the Kue Lumpur Pisang with grated coconut or a drizzle of palm sugar syrup for extra flavor and presentation.

Kue Kering Nastar (Pineapple Tart Cookies)

Ingredients:

For the Pineapple Jam Filling:

- 500 grams fresh pineapple, peeled and grated (or canned pineapple, drained and finely chopped)
- 150 grams granulated sugar (adjust according to taste)
- 1 cinnamon stick (optional)
- 2 cloves (optional)

For the Pastry Dough:

- 250 grams unsalted butter, softened
- 50 grams powdered sugar
- 2 egg yolks
- 1/2 teaspoon vanilla extract
- 300 grams all-purpose flour
- 50 grams cornstarch
- 1/4 teaspoon salt

For Egg Wash:

- 1 egg yolk
- 1 tablespoon milk or water

Instructions:

Prepare the Pineapple Jam Filling:
- In a large pan, combine the grated pineapple, granulated sugar, cinnamon stick, and cloves (if using). Cook over medium heat, stirring frequently, until the mixture thickens and turns golden brown. Remove the cinnamon stick and cloves. Allow the jam to cool completely before using.

Prepare the Pastry Dough:
- In a mixing bowl, cream together the softened butter and powdered sugar until light and fluffy.

- Add the egg yolks and vanilla extract to the butter-sugar mixture, and beat until well combined.
- Sift together the all-purpose flour, cornstarch, and salt. Gradually add the dry ingredients to the butter mixture, mixing until a soft dough forms.

Assemble the Nastar Cookies:
- Preheat your oven to 170°C (340°F). Line a baking sheet with parchment paper.
- Take a small portion of the pastry dough and flatten it in your palm. Place a small amount of pineapple jam in the center, then enclose it with the dough and roll it into a small ball.
- Place the filled dough balls onto the prepared baking sheet, leaving some space between each cookie.

Brush the cookies with egg wash:
- In a small bowl, whisk together the egg yolk and milk or water. Brush the tops of the cookies lightly with the egg wash using a pastry brush.

Bake the Nastar Cookies:
- Bake in the preheated oven for about 15-20 minutes, or until the cookies are golden brown and cooked through.

Let the cookies cool:
- Remove the cookies from the oven and let them cool on the baking sheet for a few minutes before transferring them to a wire rack to cool completely.

Serve and Enjoy:
- Once cooled, serve the Pineapple Tart Cookies and enjoy their buttery pastry and sweet pineapple filling. Store any leftovers in an airtight container to maintain freshness.

These Pineapple Tart Cookies are perfect for sharing with family and friends during festive gatherings or as a sweet snack any time of the year. Enjoy!

Kue Lumpur Coklat (Chocolate Mud Cake)

Ingredients:

- 200g unsalted butter, chopped
- 200g dark chocolate, chopped
- 1 cup (200g) brown sugar
- 1 cup (250ml) water
- 1 1/2 cups (225g) all-purpose flour
- 1/4 cup (25g) cocoa powder
- 1 teaspoon baking powder
- 1/2 teaspoon baking soda
- 2 eggs, lightly beaten
- 1 teaspoon vanilla extract
- Optional: powdered sugar or cocoa powder, for dusting

Instructions:

Preheat your oven to 160°C (320°F). Grease and line a 9-inch round cake pan with parchment paper.
In a large saucepan, combine the chopped butter, chopped dark chocolate, brown sugar, and water. Heat over low heat, stirring constantly, until the mixture is smooth and well combined. Remove from heat and allow to cool slightly.
In a large mixing bowl, sift together the all-purpose flour, cocoa powder, baking powder, and baking soda. Stir until well combined.
Gradually add the cooled chocolate mixture to the dry ingredients, stirring until smooth and well incorporated.
Add the lightly beaten eggs and vanilla extract to the batter, stirring until smooth.
Pour the batter into the prepared cake pan and smooth the top with a spatula.
Bake in the preheated oven for 50-60 minutes, or until a skewer inserted into the center of the cake comes out clean.
Remove the cake from the oven and allow it to cool in the pan for 10 minutes before transferring it to a wire rack to cool completely.
Once cooled, dust the top of the cake with powdered sugar or cocoa powder, if desired, for decoration.
Slice and serve the Chocolate Mud Cake on its own or with a dollop of whipped cream or a scoop of vanilla ice cream for an extra indulgent treat.

Enjoy the rich and decadent Chocolate Mud Cake with friends and family, savoring every bite of its moist and chocolatey goodness!
Store any leftover cake in an airtight container at room temperature for up to 3-4 days, or in the refrigerator for longer shelf life.

This Chocolate Mud Cake is perfect for special occasions or whenever you're craving a luxurious chocolate dessert. Enjoy!

Kue Lumpur Pandan (Pandan Mud Cake)

Ingredients:

- 200 grams pandan leaves, washed and chopped
- 200 ml water
- 200 grams unsalted butter, softened
- 200 grams granulated sugar
- 2 eggs
- 200 grams all-purpose flour
- 1 teaspoon baking powder
- 1/4 teaspoon salt
- 100 ml coconut milk
- Banana leaves or parchment paper, for lining the baking pan

Instructions:

Preheat your oven to 180°C (350°F). Grease a baking dish or cake pan with butter or cooking spray, and line it with banana leaves or parchment paper for easy removal.
In a blender or food processor, combine the chopped pandan leaves and water. Blend until the pandan leaves are finely chopped and the mixture turns green.
Strain the pandan mixture through a fine sieve or cheesecloth, pressing down to extract as much liquid as possible. Set aside the pandan juice.
In a mixing bowl, cream together the softened butter and granulated sugar until light and fluffy.
Add the eggs to the butter-sugar mixture, one at a time, beating well after each addition.
In a separate bowl, sift together the all-purpose flour, baking powder, and salt. Gradually add the dry ingredients to the butter mixture, alternating with the pandan juice and coconut milk. Mix until well combined and smooth.
Pour the batter into the prepared baking dish, spreading it out evenly.
Bake in the preheated oven for about 45-60 minutes, or until the top is set and golden brown, and a toothpick inserted into the center comes out clean.
Once baked, remove the Kue Lumpur Pandan from the oven and let it cool in the pan for about 10-15 minutes.
Once cooled slightly, carefully invert the Kue Lumpur Pandan onto a serving plate and remove the banana leaves or parchment paper.
Allow the cake to cool completely before slicing and serving.

Slice the Pandan Mud Cake into squares or rectangles, and serve it as a delicious dessert or snack.

Enjoy the fragrant and moist Pandan Mud Cake with family and friends, savoring its unique flavor and vibrant green color!

Store any leftover cake in an airtight container in the refrigerator for up to 3-4 days. You can reheat it in the microwave for a few seconds before serving to enjoy it warm.

Feel free to garnish the Pandan Mud Cake with grated coconut or a drizzle of condensed milk for extra flavor and presentation.

Kue Lumpur Tape (Fermented Cassava Mud Cake)

Ingredients:

- 500 grams fermented cassava (tape), mashed
- 200 ml coconut milk
- 150 grams granulated sugar
- 100 grams rice flour
- 1/4 teaspoon salt
- Banana leaves or parchment paper, for lining the baking pan

Instructions:

Preheat your oven to 180°C (350°F). Grease a baking dish or cake pan with butter or cooking spray, and line it with banana leaves or parchment paper for easy removal.
In a mixing bowl, combine the mashed fermented cassava, coconut milk, granulated sugar, rice flour, and salt. Mix well until the ingredients are evenly incorporated and the batter is smooth.
Pour the batter into the prepared baking dish, spreading it out evenly.
Bake in the preheated oven for about 45-60 minutes, or until the top is set and golden brown, and a toothpick inserted into the center comes out clean.
Once baked, remove the Kue Lumpur Tape from the oven and let it cool in the pan for about 10-15 minutes.
Once cooled slightly, carefully invert the Kue Lumpur Tape onto a serving plate and remove the banana leaves or parchment paper.
Allow the cake to cool completely before slicing and serving.
Slice the Kue Lumpur Tape into squares or rectangles, and serve it as a delicious dessert or snack.
Enjoy the unique flavor and texture of the Fermented Cassava Mud Cake with family and friends!
Store any leftover cake in an airtight container in the refrigerator for up to 3-4 days. You can reheat it in the microwave for a few seconds before serving to enjoy it warm.

Feel free to garnish the Kue Lumpur Tape with grated coconut or a drizzle of palm sugar syrup for extra flavor and presentation.

Kue Lumpur Keju (Cheese Mud Cake)

Ingredients:

- 200g unsalted butter, chopped
- 200g dark chocolate, chopped
- 1 cup (200g) brown sugar
- 1 cup (250ml) water
- 1 cup (120g) all-purpose flour
- 1/4 cup (25g) cocoa powder
- 1 teaspoon baking powder
- 1/2 teaspoon baking soda
- 2 eggs, lightly beaten
- 1 teaspoon vanilla extract
- 100g grated cheddar cheese (or cheese of your choice)
- Optional: powdered sugar, for dusting

Instructions:

Preheat your oven to 160°C (320°F). Grease and line a 9-inch round cake pan with parchment paper.

In a large saucepan, combine the chopped butter, chopped dark chocolate, brown sugar, and water. Heat over low heat, stirring constantly, until the mixture is smooth and well combined. Remove from heat and allow to cool slightly.

In a large mixing bowl, sift together the all-purpose flour, cocoa powder, baking powder, and baking soda. Stir until well combined.

Gradually add the cooled chocolate mixture to the dry ingredients, stirring until smooth and well incorporated.

Add the lightly beaten eggs and vanilla extract to the batter, stirring until smooth.

Fold in the grated cheddar cheese until evenly distributed throughout the batter.

Pour the batter into the prepared cake pan and smooth the top with a spatula.

Bake in the preheated oven for 50-60 minutes, or until a skewer inserted into the center of the cake comes out clean.

Remove the cake from the oven and allow it to cool in the pan for 10 minutes before transferring it to a wire rack to cool completely.

Once cooled, dust the top of the cake with powdered sugar, if desired, for decoration.

Slice and serve the Cheese Mud Cake on its own or with a dollop of whipped cream or a scoop of vanilla ice cream for an extra indulgent treat.
Enjoy the rich and decadent Cheese Mud Cake with friends and family, savoring every bite of its moist and chocolatey goodness!
Store any leftover cake in an airtight container at room temperature for up to 3-4 days, or in the refrigerator for longer shelf life.

This Cheese Mud Cake is perfect for special occasions or whenever you're craving a luxurious chocolate dessert with a cheesy twist. Enjoy!

Kue Lumpur Keju Coklat (Chocolate Cheese Mud Cake)

Ingredients:

- 200g unsalted butter, chopped
- 200g dark chocolate, chopped
- 1 cup (200g) brown sugar
- 1 cup (250ml) water
- 1 cup (120g) all-purpose flour
- 1/4 cup (25g) cocoa powder
- 1 teaspoon baking powder
- 1/2 teaspoon baking soda
- 2 eggs, lightly beaten
- 1 teaspoon vanilla extract
- 100g grated cheddar cheese (or cheese of your choice)
- Optional: powdered sugar, for dusting

Instructions:

Preheat your oven to 160°C (320°F). Grease and line a 9-inch round cake pan with parchment paper.

In a large saucepan, combine the chopped butter, chopped dark chocolate, brown sugar, and water. Heat over low heat, stirring constantly, until the mixture is smooth and well combined. Remove from heat and allow to cool slightly.

In a large mixing bowl, sift together the all-purpose flour, cocoa powder, baking powder, and baking soda. Stir until well combined.

Gradually add the cooled chocolate mixture to the dry ingredients, stirring until smooth and well incorporated.

Add the lightly beaten eggs and vanilla extract to the batter, stirring until smooth.

Fold in the grated cheddar cheese until evenly distributed throughout the batter.

Pour the batter into the prepared cake pan and smooth the top with a spatula.

Bake in the preheated oven for 50-60 minutes, or until a skewer inserted into the center of the cake comes out clean.

Remove the cake from the oven and allow it to cool in the pan for 10 minutes before transferring it to a wire rack to cool completely.

Once cooled, dust the top of the cake with powdered sugar, if desired, for decoration.

Slice and serve the Chocolate Cheese Mud Cake on its own or with a dollop of whipped cream or a scoop of vanilla ice cream for an extra indulgent treat.

Enjoy the rich and decadent Chocolate Cheese Mud Cake with friends and family, savoring every bite of its moist and chocolatey goodness!

Store any leftover cake in an airtight container at room temperature for up to 3-4 days, or in the refrigerator for longer shelf life.

This Chocolate Cheese Mud Cake is sure to be a hit at any gathering or special occasion. Enjoy!

Bolu Kukus (Steamed Sponge Cake)

Ingredients:

- 200 grams all-purpose flour
- 150 grams granulated sugar
- 3 eggs
- 1 teaspoon baking powder
- 1/4 teaspoon salt
- 1 teaspoon vanilla extract
- 100 ml coconut milk
- 1 tablespoon melted butter or vegetable oil, for greasing
- Optional: grated cheese, chocolate chips, or raisins for topping

Instructions:

Prepare your steamer by filling it with water and bringing it to a simmer over medium heat.
In a mixing bowl, beat the eggs and sugar together until light and fluffy.
Add the vanilla extract and salt to the egg mixture and mix until well combined.
Sift the all-purpose flour and baking powder into the egg mixture. Gently fold the dry ingredients into the wet ingredients until just combined. Do not overmix.
Gradually pour in the coconut milk while stirring continuously until the batter is smooth and well combined.
Grease your cake molds or muffin tins with melted butter or vegetable oil.
Pour the batter into the greased molds, filling each mold about 3/4 full.
If desired, sprinkle grated cheese, chocolate chips, or raisins on top of the batter.
Place the filled molds into the steamer basket, making sure they are not touching each other.
Steam the Bolu Kukus over medium heat for about 20-25 minutes, or until a toothpick inserted into the center of the cake comes out clean.
Once cooked, remove the Bolu Kukus from the steamer and let them cool slightly before removing them from the molds.
Serve the Steamed Sponge Cakes warm or at room temperature. Enjoy them as a delightful snack or dessert with your favorite beverage.
Store any leftover Bolu Kukus in an airtight container at room temperature for up to 2-3 days. They can also be stored in the refrigerator for longer shelf life.

This Bolu Kukus recipe is versatile, and you can customize it by adding your favorite toppings or flavors. Whether enjoyed plain or with added toppings, Bolu Kukus is sure to delight your taste buds with its soft and fluffy texture.

Kue Lumpur Ubi (Sweet Potato Mud Cake)

Ingredients:

- 500 grams sweet potatoes, peeled and cubed
- 200 ml coconut milk
- 150 grams granulated sugar
- 200 grams all-purpose flour
- 1 teaspoon baking powder
- 1/4 teaspoon salt
- Banana leaves or parchment paper, for lining the baking pan

Instructions:

Preheat your oven to 180°C (350°F). Grease a baking dish or cake pan with butter or cooking spray, and line it with banana leaves or parchment paper for easy removal.
Boil the sweet potatoes in a pot of water until they are soft and tender, about 15-20 minutes. Drain the sweet potatoes and mash them with a fork or potato masher until smooth. Let them cool slightly.
In a mixing bowl, combine the mashed sweet potatoes, coconut milk, and granulated sugar. Mix well until the sugar is dissolved and the mixture is smooth.
In another bowl, sift together the all-purpose flour, baking powder, and salt. Gradually add the dry ingredients to the sweet potato mixture, stirring until well combined.
Pour the batter into the prepared baking dish, spreading it out evenly.
Bake in the preheated oven for about 45-60 minutes, or until the top is set and golden brown, and a toothpick inserted into the center comes out clean.
Once baked, remove the Kue Lumpur Ubi from the oven and let it cool in the pan for about 10-15 minutes.
Once cooled slightly, carefully invert the Kue Lumpur Ubi onto a serving plate and remove the banana leaves or parchment paper.
Allow the cake to cool completely before slicing and serving.
Slice the Sweet Potato Mud Cake into squares or rectangles, and serve it as a delicious dessert or snack.
Enjoy the rich and moist Sweet Potato Mud Cake with family and friends, savoring its unique flavor and texture!

Store any leftover cake in an airtight container in the refrigerator for up to 3-4 days. You can reheat it in the microwave for a few seconds before serving to enjoy it warm.

Feel free to garnish the Sweet Potato Mud Cake with grated coconut or a drizzle of condensed milk for extra flavor and presentation.

Kue Lumpur Nangka (Jackfruit Mud Cake)

Ingredients:

- 200 grams ripe jackfruit flesh, mashed
- 200 ml coconut milk
- 150 grams granulated sugar
- 200 grams all-purpose flour
- 1 teaspoon baking powder
- 1/4 teaspoon salt
- Banana leaves or parchment paper, for lining the baking pan

Instructions:

Preheat your oven to 180°C (350°F). Grease a baking dish or cake pan with butter or cooking spray, and line it with banana leaves or parchment paper for easy removal.
In a mixing bowl, combine the mashed ripe jackfruit flesh, coconut milk, and granulated sugar. Mix well until the sugar is dissolved and the mixture is smooth.
In another bowl, sift together the all-purpose flour, baking powder, and salt.
Gradually add the dry ingredients to the jackfruit mixture, stirring until well combined.
Pour the batter into the prepared baking dish, spreading it out evenly.
Bake in the preheated oven for about 45-60 minutes, or until the top is set and golden brown, and a toothpick inserted into the center comes out clean.
Once baked, remove the Kue Lumpur Nangka from the oven and let it cool in the pan for about 10-15 minutes.
Once cooled slightly, carefully invert the Kue Lumpur Nangka onto a serving plate and remove the banana leaves or parchment paper.
Allow the cake to cool completely before slicing and serving.
Slice the Jackfruit Mud Cake into squares or rectangles, and serve it as a delicious dessert or snack.
Enjoy the rich and flavorful Jackfruit Mud Cake with family and friends, savoring its unique tropical taste!
Store any leftover cake in an airtight container in the refrigerator for up to 3-4 days. You can reheat it in the microwave for a few seconds before serving to enjoy it warm.

Feel free to garnish the Jackfruit Mud Cake with additional pieces of jackfruit or a sprinkle of powdered sugar for extra sweetness and presentation.

Kue Lumpur Ubi Ungu (Purple Sweet Potato Mud Cake)

Ingredients:

- 500 grams purple sweet potatoes, peeled and cubed
- 200 ml coconut milk
- 150 grams granulated sugar
- 200 grams all-purpose flour
- 1 teaspoon baking powder
- 1/4 teaspoon salt
- Banana leaves or parchment paper, for lining the baking pan

Instructions:

Preheat your oven to 180°C (350°F). Grease a baking dish or cake pan with butter or cooking spray, and line it with banana leaves or parchment paper for easy removal.

Boil the purple sweet potatoes in a pot of water until they are soft and tender, about 15-20 minutes. Drain the sweet potatoes and mash them with a fork or potato masher until smooth. Let them cool slightly.

In a mixing bowl, combine the mashed purple sweet potatoes, coconut milk, and granulated sugar. Mix well until the sugar is dissolved and the mixture is smooth.

In another bowl, sift together the all-purpose flour, baking powder, and salt. Gradually add the dry ingredients to the sweet potato mixture, stirring until well combined.

Pour the batter into the prepared baking dish, spreading it out evenly.

Bake in the preheated oven for about 45-60 minutes, or until the top is set and golden brown, and a toothpick inserted into the center comes out clean.

Once baked, remove the Kue Lumpur Ubi Ungu from the oven and let it cool in the pan for about 10-15 minutes.

Once cooled slightly, carefully invert the Kue Lumpur Ubi Ungu onto a serving plate and remove the banana leaves or parchment paper.

Allow the cake to cool completely before slicing and serving.

Slice the Purple Sweet Potato Mud Cake into squares or rectangles, and serve it as a delicious dessert or snack.

Enjoy the rich and moist Purple Sweet Potato Mud Cake with family and friends, savoring its unique color and flavor!

Store any leftover cake in an airtight container in the refrigerator for up to 3-4 days. You can reheat it in the microwave for a few seconds before serving to enjoy it warm.

Feel free to garnish the Purple Sweet Potato Mud Cake with additional purple sweet potato slices or a sprinkle of powdered sugar for extra sweetness and presentation.

Kue Lumpur Durian (Durian Mud Cake)

Ingredients:

- 500 grams durian flesh, fresh or frozen
- 200 ml coconut milk
- 150 grams granulated sugar
- 200 grams all-purpose flour
- 1 teaspoon baking powder
- 1/4 teaspoon salt
- Banana leaves or parchment paper, for lining the baking pan

Instructions:

Preheat your oven to 180°C (350°F). Grease a baking dish or cake pan with butter or cooking spray, and line it with banana leaves or parchment paper for easy removal.

If using fresh durian, remove the flesh from the durian pods and discard the seeds. If using frozen durian, thaw it according to package instructions.

In a mixing bowl, mash the durian flesh with a fork or potato masher until smooth.

Add the coconut milk and granulated sugar to the mashed durian flesh. Mix well until the sugar is dissolved and the mixture is smooth.

In another bowl, sift together the all-purpose flour, baking powder, and salt. Gradually add the dry ingredients to the durian mixture, stirring until well combined.

Pour the batter into the prepared baking dish, spreading it out evenly.

Bake in the preheated oven for about 45-60 minutes, or until the top is set and golden brown, and a toothpick inserted into the center comes out clean.

Once baked, remove the Kue Lumpur Durian from the oven and let it cool in the pan for about 10-15 minutes.

Once cooled slightly, carefully invert the Kue Lumpur Durian onto a serving plate and remove the banana leaves or parchment paper.

Allow the cake to cool completely before slicing and serving.

Slice the Durian Mud Cake into squares or rectangles, and serve it as a delicious dessert or snack.

Enjoy the rich and flavorful Durian Mud Cake with family and friends, savoring its unique taste and aroma!

Store any leftover cake in an airtight container in the refrigerator for up to 3-4 days. You can reheat it in the microwave for a few seconds before serving to enjoy it warm.

Feel free to garnish the Durian Mud Cake with additional pieces of durian or a sprinkle of powdered sugar for extra sweetness and presentation.

Kue Lumpur Labu (Pumpkin Mud Cake)

Ingredients:

- 500 grams pumpkin, peeled and cubed
- 200 ml coconut milk
- 150 grams granulated sugar
- 200 grams all-purpose flour
- 1 teaspoon baking powder
- 1/4 teaspoon salt
- Banana leaves or parchment paper, for lining the baking pan

Instructions:

Preheat your oven to 180°C (350°F). Grease a baking dish or cake pan with butter or cooking spray, and line it with banana leaves or parchment paper for easy removal.

Boil the pumpkin cubes in a pot of water until they are soft and tender, about 10-15 minutes. Drain the pumpkin and mash it with a fork or potato masher until smooth. Let it cool slightly.

In a mixing bowl, combine the mashed pumpkin, coconut milk, and granulated sugar. Mix well until the sugar is dissolved and the mixture is smooth.

In another bowl, sift together the all-purpose flour, baking powder, and salt. Gradually add the dry ingredients to the pumpkin mixture, stirring until well combined.

Pour the batter into the prepared baking dish, spreading it out evenly.

Bake in the preheated oven for about 45-60 minutes, or until the top is set and golden brown, and a toothpick inserted into the center comes out clean.

Once baked, remove the Kue Lumpur Labu from the oven and let it cool in the pan for about 10-15 minutes.

Once cooled slightly, carefully invert the Pumpkin Mud Cake onto a serving plate and remove the banana leaves or parchment paper.

Allow the cake to cool completely before slicing and serving.

Slice the Pumpkin Mud Cake into squares or rectangles, and serve it as a delicious dessert or snack.

Enjoy the rich and moist Pumpkin Mud Cake with family and friends, savoring its delightful pumpkin flavor!

Store any leftover cake in an airtight container in the refrigerator for up to 3-4 days. You can reheat it in the microwave for a few seconds before serving to enjoy it warm.

Feel free to garnish the Pumpkin Mud Cake with a sprinkle of cinnamon or powdered sugar for extra flavor and presentation.

Kue Lumpur Pisang Keju (Banana Cheese Mud Cake)

Ingredients:

- 3 ripe bananas, mashed
- 200 grams grated cheese (cheddar or any cheese of your choice)
- 200 ml coconut milk
- 150 grams granulated sugar
- 200 grams all-purpose flour
- 1 teaspoon baking powder
- 1/4 teaspoon salt
- Banana leaves or parchment paper, for lining the baking pan

Instructions:

Preheat your oven to 180°C (350°F). Grease a baking dish or cake pan with butter or cooking spray, and line it with banana leaves or parchment paper for easy removal.

In a mixing bowl, combine the mashed ripe bananas, grated cheese, coconut milk, and granulated sugar. Mix well until the sugar is dissolved and the mixture is smooth.

In another bowl, sift together the all-purpose flour, baking powder, and salt. Gradually add the dry ingredients to the banana mixture, stirring until well combined.

Pour the batter into the prepared baking dish, spreading it out evenly.

Bake in the preheated oven for about 45-60 minutes, or until the top is set and golden brown, and a toothpick inserted into the center comes out clean.

Once baked, remove the Kue Lumpur Pisang Keju from the oven and let it cool in the pan for about 10-15 minutes.

Once cooled slightly, carefully invert the Banana Cheese Mud Cake onto a serving plate and remove the banana leaves or parchment paper.

Allow the cake to cool completely before slicing and serving.

Slice the Banana Cheese Mud Cake into squares or rectangles, and serve it as a delicious dessert or snack.

Enjoy the rich and flavorful Banana Cheese Mud Cake with family and friends, savoring its delightful combination of banana and cheese!

Store any leftover cake in an airtight container in the refrigerator for up to 3-4 days. You can reheat it in the microwave for a few seconds before serving to enjoy it warm.

Feel free to garnish the Banana Cheese Mud Cake with additional grated cheese or sliced bananas for extra flavor and presentation.

Kue Lumpur Nenas (Pineapple Mud Cake)

Ingredients:

- 1 can (20 oz) crushed pineapple, drained
- 200 ml coconut milk
- 150 grams granulated sugar
- 200 grams all-purpose flour
- 1 teaspoon baking powder
- 1/4 teaspoon salt
- Banana leaves or parchment paper, for lining the baking pan

Instructions:

Preheat your oven to 180°C (350°F). Grease a baking dish or cake pan with butter or cooking spray, and line it with banana leaves or parchment paper for easy removal.
In a mixing bowl, combine the drained crushed pineapple, coconut milk, and granulated sugar. Mix well until the sugar is dissolved and the mixture is smooth.
In another bowl, sift together the all-purpose flour, baking powder, and salt.
Gradually add the dry ingredients to the pineapple mixture, stirring until well combined.
Pour the batter into the prepared baking dish, spreading it out evenly.
Bake in the preheated oven for about 45-60 minutes, or until the top is set and golden brown, and a toothpick inserted into the center comes out clean.
Once baked, remove the Kue Lumpur Nenas from the oven and let it cool in the pan for about 10-15 minutes.
Once cooled slightly, carefully invert the Pineapple Mud Cake onto a serving plate and remove the banana leaves or parchment paper.
Allow the cake to cool completely before slicing and serving.
Slice the Pineapple Mud Cake into squares or rectangles, and serve it as a delicious dessert or snack.
Enjoy the tangy sweetness of the Pineapple Mud Cake with family and friends, savoring its unique flavor!
Store any leftover cake in an airtight container in the refrigerator for up to 3-4 days. You can reheat it in the microwave for a few seconds before serving to enjoy it warm.

Feel free to garnish the Pineapple Mud Cake with additional pineapple slices or a sprinkle of powdered sugar for extra flavor and presentation.

Kue Lumpur Stroberi (Strawberry Mud Cake)

Ingredients:

- 200 grams fresh strawberries, hulled and chopped
- 200 ml coconut milk
- 150 grams granulated sugar
- 200 grams all-purpose flour
- 1 teaspoon baking powder
- 1/4 teaspoon salt
- Banana leaves or parchment paper, for lining the baking pan

Instructions:

Preheat your oven to 180°C (350°F). Grease a baking dish or cake pan with butter or cooking spray, and line it with banana leaves or parchment paper for easy removal.
In a blender or food processor, puree the chopped strawberries until smooth.
In a mixing bowl, combine the strawberry puree, coconut milk, and granulated sugar. Mix well until the sugar is dissolved and the mixture is smooth.
In another bowl, sift together the all-purpose flour, baking powder, and salt.
Gradually add the dry ingredients to the strawberry mixture, stirring until well combined.
Pour the batter into the prepared baking dish, spreading it out evenly.
Bake in the preheated oven for about 45-60 minutes, or until the top is set and golden brown, and a toothpick inserted into the center comes out clean.
Once baked, remove the Kue Lumpur Stroberi from the oven and let it cool in the pan for about 10-15 minutes.
Once cooled slightly, carefully invert the Strawberry Mud Cake onto a serving plate and remove the banana leaves or parchment paper.
Allow the cake to cool completely before slicing and serving.
Slice the Strawberry Mud Cake into squares or rectangles, and serve it as a delicious dessert or snack.
Enjoy the sweet and tangy flavor of the Strawberry Mud Cake with family and friends, savoring its delightful taste!
Store any leftover cake in an airtight container in the refrigerator for up to 3-4 days. You can reheat it in the microwave for a few seconds before serving to enjoy it warm.

Feel free to garnish the Strawberry Mud Cake with fresh strawberry slices or a dollop of whipped cream for extra flavor and presentation.

Kue Lumpur Anggur (Grape Mud Cake)

Ingredients:

- 200 grams seedless grapes (red or green), washed and halved
- 200 ml coconut milk
- 150 grams granulated sugar
- 200 grams all-purpose flour
- 1 teaspoon baking powder
- 1/4 teaspoon salt
- Banana leaves or parchment paper, for lining the baking pan

Instructions:

Preheat your oven to 180°C (350°F). Grease a baking dish or cake pan with butter or cooking spray, and line it with banana leaves or parchment paper for easy removal.
In a mixing bowl, combine the halved grapes, coconut milk, and granulated sugar. Mix well until the sugar is dissolved and the mixture is smooth.
In another bowl, sift together the all-purpose flour, baking powder, and salt. Gradually add the dry ingredients to the grape mixture, stirring until well combined.
Pour the batter into the prepared baking dish, spreading it out evenly.
Bake in the preheated oven for about 45-60 minutes, or until the top is set and golden brown, and a toothpick inserted into the center comes out clean.
Once baked, remove the Kue Lumpur Anggur from the oven and let it cool in the pan for about 10-15 minutes.
Once cooled slightly, carefully invert the Grape Mud Cake onto a serving plate and remove the banana leaves or parchment paper.
Allow the cake to cool completely before slicing and serving.
Slice the Grape Mud Cake into squares or rectangles, and serve it as a delicious dessert or snack.
Enjoy the sweet and juicy flavor of the Grape Mud Cake with family and friends, savoring its delightful taste!
Store any leftover cake in an airtight container in the refrigerator for up to 3-4 days. You can reheat it in the microwave for a few seconds before serving to enjoy it warm.

Feel free to garnish the Grape Mud Cake with additional grape halves or a sprinkle of powdered sugar for extra flavor and presentation.

Kue Lumpur Mangga (Mango Mud Cake)

Ingredients:

- 2 ripe mangoes, peeled and diced
- 200 ml coconut milk
- 150 grams granulated sugar
- 200 grams all-purpose flour
- 1 teaspoon baking powder
- 1/4 teaspoon salt
- Banana leaves or parchment paper, for lining the baking pan

Instructions:

Preheat your oven to 180°C (350°F). Grease a baking dish or cake pan with butter or cooking spray, and line it with banana leaves or parchment paper for easy removal.
In a blender or food processor, puree one of the diced mangoes until smooth.
In a mixing bowl, combine the mango puree, coconut milk, and granulated sugar. Mix well until the sugar is dissolved and the mixture is smooth.
In another bowl, sift together the all-purpose flour, baking powder, and salt. Gradually add the dry ingredients to the mango mixture, stirring until well combined.
Fold in the remaining diced mango into the batter, mixing until evenly distributed.
Pour the batter into the prepared baking dish, spreading it out evenly.
Bake in the preheated oven for about 45-60 minutes, or until the top is set and golden brown, and a toothpick inserted into the center comes out clean.
Once baked, remove the Kue Lumpur Mangga from the oven and let it cool in the pan for about 10-15 minutes.
Once cooled slightly, carefully invert the Mango Mud Cake onto a serving plate and remove the banana leaves or parchment paper.
Allow the cake to cool completely before slicing and serving.
Slice the Mango Mud Cake into squares or rectangles, and serve it as a delicious dessert or snack.
Enjoy the tropical sweetness of the Mango Mud Cake with family and friends, savoring its delightful taste!

Store any leftover cake in an airtight container in the refrigerator for up to 3-4 days. You can reheat it in the microwave for a few seconds before serving to enjoy it warm.

Feel free to garnish the Mango Mud Cake with additional diced mangoes or a sprinkle of shredded coconut for extra flavor and presentation.

Kue Lumpur Tiramisu (Tiramisu Mud Cake)

Ingredients:

For the Cake:

- 200 ml strong brewed coffee, cooled
- 200 ml coconut milk
- 150 grams granulated sugar
- 200 grams all-purpose flour
- 1 teaspoon baking powder
- 1/4 teaspoon salt

For the Tiramisu Filling:

- 250 grams mascarpone cheese, softened
- 100 grams powdered sugar
- 1 teaspoon vanilla extract

For Garnish:

- Cocoa powder, for dusting
- Chocolate shavings or cocoa nibs, optional

Instructions:

Preheat your oven to 180°C (350°F). Grease a baking dish or cake pan with butter or cooking spray, and line it with parchment paper for easy removal.
In a mixing bowl, combine the cooled brewed coffee, coconut milk, and granulated sugar. Mix well until the sugar is dissolved.
In another bowl, sift together the all-purpose flour, baking powder, and salt. Gradually add the dry ingredients to the coffee mixture, stirring until well combined.
Pour the batter into the prepared baking dish, spreading it out evenly.
Bake in the preheated oven for about 45-60 minutes, or until the top is set and golden brown, and a toothpick inserted into the center comes out clean.

Once baked, remove the cake from the oven and let it cool in the pan for about 10-15 minutes.

While the cake is cooling, prepare the Tiramisu filling. In a mixing bowl, combine the softened mascarpone cheese, powdered sugar, and vanilla extract. Mix until smooth and well combined.

Once the cake has cooled slightly, carefully remove it from the pan and transfer it to a serving plate or cake stand.

Using a serrated knife, slice the cake horizontally into two even layers.

Spread a layer of the prepared Tiramisu filling on top of one of the cake layers.

Place the second cake layer on top of the filling, creating a sandwich.

Spread the remaining Tiramisu filling evenly over the top of the cake.

Dust the top of the cake with cocoa powder, and garnish with chocolate shavings or cocoa nibs if desired.

Refrigerate the Tiramisu Mud Cake for at least 1-2 hours before serving to allow the flavors to meld together.

Slice and serve the Tiramisu Mud Cake chilled, and enjoy its rich, decadent flavors!

Store any leftover cake in an airtight container in the refrigerator for up to 3-4 days.

This Tiramisu Mud Cake is sure to impress with its delicious combination of coffee, cocoa, and creamy mascarpone filling. Enjoy it as a dessert for special occasions or whenever you're craving a decadent treat!

Klepon Ketan (Sticky Rice Cake Balls)

Ingredients:

For the Filling:

- 100 grams palm sugar (gula melaka), chopped into small pieces
- 50 grams grated coconut (fresh or desiccated)

For the Dough:

- 200 grams glutinous rice flour
- 1 pandan leaf (optional), knotted
- 100 ml water
- 1-2 drops green food coloring (optional)

For Coating:

- 100 grams grated coconut (fresh or desiccated)

Instructions:

Prepare the Filling:
- In a small bowl, mix the chopped palm sugar with grated coconut until well combined. Set aside.

Prepare the Dough:
- In a mixing bowl, combine the glutinous rice flour and pandan leaf (if using). Gradually add water while kneading until you get a smooth, pliable dough.
- Add green food coloring (if using) to achieve the desired color. Knead until the color is evenly distributed.

Assemble the Klepon:
- Pinch off a small piece of dough and flatten it in your palm. Place a small amount of the palm sugar filling in the center.
- Carefully enclose the filling with the dough, shaping it into a small ball. Ensure the filling is completely covered with dough to prevent leakage during cooking.

- Repeat the process until all the dough and filling are used up.

Cook the Klepon:
- Bring a pot of water to a gentle boil over medium heat.
- Carefully drop the Klepon into the boiling water, a few at a time, to avoid overcrowding the pot.
- Cook the Klepon until they float to the surface, indicating they are cooked, about 2-3 minutes.
- Using a slotted spoon, remove the cooked Klepon from the water and drain off any excess water.

Coat the Klepon:
- Roll the cooked Klepon in grated coconut while they are still warm, ensuring they are evenly coated.

Serve:
- Arrange the Klepon on a serving plate and serve them warm or at room temperature.

Enjoy:
- Bite into the soft, chewy Klepon to reveal the oozing palm sugar filling and savor the combination of flavors and textures.

Storage:
- Klepon is best enjoyed fresh on the day it is made. However, you can store any leftovers in an airtight container in the refrigerator for up to 2 days. Reheat gently before serving.

These Klepon Ketan are a delightful treat that captures the essence of Indonesian sweets with their fragrant pandan aroma, sweet palm sugar filling, and chewy texture. Enjoy making and sharing them with family and friends!

Kue Lapis Legit Prune (Prune Layer Cake)

Ingredients:

- 250 grams butter, softened
- 200 grams granulated sugar
- 8 eggs, separated
- 150 grams all-purpose flour
- 100 grams prune puree (cooked and mashed prunes)
- 1/2 teaspoon cinnamon powder
- 1/4 teaspoon nutmeg powder
- 1/4 teaspoon clove powder
- Butter or cooking spray, for greasing the pan
- Prune slices, for garnish (optional)

Instructions:

Preheat your oven to 180°C (350°F). Grease a 20 cm (8-inch) round cake pan with butter or cooking spray and line the bottom with parchment paper.
In a large mixing bowl, cream together the softened butter and granulated sugar until light and fluffy.
Add the egg yolks one at a time, beating well after each addition, until fully incorporated.
Sift the all-purpose flour into the batter and mix until smooth.
In a separate clean mixing bowl, beat the egg whites until stiff peaks form.
Gently fold the beaten egg whites into the cake batter until well combined.
Divide the batter into two equal portions.
In one portion of the batter, fold in the prune puree until evenly distributed.
Add the cinnamon powder, nutmeg powder, and clove powder to the other portion of the batter and mix until well combined.
Pour a thin layer of the prune batter into the prepared cake pan and spread it evenly.
Place the cake pan in the preheated oven and bake for about 8-10 minutes, or until the layer is set and lightly golden brown.
Remove the cake pan from the oven and carefully pour a thin layer of the spiced batter over the baked prune layer. Spread it evenly.
Return the cake pan to the oven and bake for another 8-10 minutes, or until the layer is set and lightly golden brown.

Continue alternating between the prune and spiced batters, pouring and baking each layer until all the batter is used up. Make sure to spread each layer evenly. Once all layers are baked, remove the cake from the oven and let it cool completely in the pan.

Once cooled, remove the cake from the pan and slice it into squares or rectangles.

Garnish the Kue Lapis Legit Prune with prune slices if desired.

Serve and enjoy this delicious and aromatic Indonesian Prune Layer Cake!

Store any leftover cake in an airtight container in the refrigerator for up to 3-4 days.

This Kue Lapis Legit Prune is sure to impress with its beautiful layers and rich flavors. Enjoy making and sharing it with your loved ones!

Kue Cubit Pandan (Pandan Pancake Bites)

Ingredients:

- 200 grams all-purpose flour
- 100 grams granulated sugar
- 1 teaspoon baking powder
- 1/4 teaspoon salt
- 2 eggs
- 200 ml coconut milk
- 1 teaspoon pandan extract
- Cooking oil, for greasing the pan

Instructions:

In a mixing bowl, sift together the all-purpose flour, granulated sugar, baking powder, and salt. Mix well to combine.
In another bowl, whisk together the eggs, coconut milk, and pandan extract until well combined.
Gradually add the wet ingredients to the dry ingredients, stirring until you get a smooth batter. Ensure there are no lumps.
Heat a non-stick pan or griddle over medium heat and lightly grease it with cooking oil.
Pour small amounts of the batter onto the hot pan to form small pancakes, about 5 cm (2 inches) in diameter.
Cook the pancakes for 1-2 minutes on each side, or until they are golden brown and cooked through.
Once cooked, remove the pancakes from the pan and set them aside to cool slightly.
Repeat the process with the remaining batter, greasing the pan as needed.
Serve the Kue Cubit Pandan pancakes warm or at room temperature.
Enjoy these fluffy and aromatic Pandan Pancake Bites as a delicious snack or dessert!

Feel free to customize your Kue Cubit Pandan by topping them with chocolate chips, shredded cheese, or your favorite jam. You can also serve them with a drizzle of condensed milk for extra sweetness. These bite-sized treats are sure to be a hit with your family and friends!

Kue Lumpur Keju Jagung (Cheese Corn Mud Cake)

Ingredients:

- 200 grams corn kernels (fresh, frozen, or canned)
- 200 ml coconut milk
- 150 grams granulated sugar
- 200 grams all-purpose flour
- 1 teaspoon baking powder
- 1/4 teaspoon salt
- 100 grams grated cheese (cheddar or any cheese of your choice)
- Banana leaves or parchment paper, for lining the baking pan

Instructions:

Preheat your oven to 180°C (350°F). Grease a baking dish or cake pan with butter or cooking spray, and line it with banana leaves or parchment paper for easy removal.
If using fresh corn kernels, cook them until tender. If using frozen or canned corn kernels, thaw and drain them.
In a blender or food processor, puree half of the corn kernels with the coconut milk until smooth. Chop the remaining corn kernels into smaller pieces.
In a mixing bowl, combine the pureed corn mixture, chopped corn kernels, granulated sugar, and grated cheese. Mix well until the sugar is dissolved and the mixture is smooth.
In another bowl, sift together the all-purpose flour, baking powder, and salt.
Gradually add the dry ingredients to the corn mixture, stirring until well combined.
Pour the batter into the prepared baking dish, spreading it out evenly.
Bake in the preheated oven for about 45-60 minutes, or until the top is set and golden brown, and a toothpick inserted into the center comes out clean.
Once baked, remove the Kue Lumpur Keju Jagung from the oven and let it cool in the pan for about 10-15 minutes.
Once cooled slightly, carefully invert the Cheese Corn Mud Cake onto a serving plate and remove the banana leaves or parchment paper.
Allow the cake to cool completely before slicing and serving.
Slice the Cheese Corn Mud Cake into squares or rectangles, and serve it as a delicious dessert or snack.

Enjoy the rich and flavorful Cheese Corn Mud Cake with family and friends, savoring its delightful combination of cheese and corn!
Store any leftover cake in an airtight container in the refrigerator for up to 3-4 days. You can reheat it in the microwave for a few seconds before serving to enjoy it warm.

Feel free to garnish the Cheese Corn Mud Cake with additional grated cheese or corn kernels for extra flavor and presentation.

Risoles Sayur (Vegetable Spring Rolls)

Ingredients:

For the Filling:

- 2 tablespoons vegetable oil
- 1 small onion, finely chopped
- 2 cloves garlic, minced
- 1 carrot, finely diced
- 1 small potato, finely diced
- 1/2 cup cabbage, thinly sliced
- 1/2 cup green beans, finely chopped
- Salt and pepper to taste
- 1/2 teaspoon curry powder (optional)
- 1/2 cup chicken or vegetable broth
- 2 tablespoons all-purpose flour
- 1/2 cup milk
- 1/2 cup grated cheese (optional)
- Spring roll wrappers (store-bought or homemade)
- Breadcrumbs for coating
- Oil for frying

For the Dipping Sauce:

- Sweet chili sauce or your favorite dipping sauce

Instructions:

Heat the vegetable oil in a large pan over medium heat. Add the chopped onion and minced garlic, and sauté until fragrant and translucent.

Add the diced carrot and potato to the pan, and cook for a few minutes until slightly softened.

Stir in the sliced cabbage and chopped green beans. Season with salt, pepper, and curry powder (if using). Cook for another few minutes until the vegetables are tender.

In a small bowl, whisk together the chicken or vegetable broth and all-purpose flour until smooth. Pour the mixture into the pan, stirring constantly until it thickens.

Gradually pour in the milk while stirring continuously. Cook until the mixture thickens and coats the back of a spoon.

Add the grated cheese (if using) and stir until melted and well combined. Remove the filling from the heat and let it cool slightly.

Take a spring roll wrapper and place a spoonful of the vegetable filling in the center. Fold the bottom edge of the wrapper over the filling, then fold in the sides, and roll it tightly into a cylinder shape. Secure the end with a little water to seal the roll.

Dip the filled spring roll into breadcrumbs, ensuring it's evenly coated.

Heat oil in a deep frying pan or pot over medium heat. Once the oil is hot, carefully place the spring rolls in the oil, seam side down, and fry until golden brown and crispy, turning occasionally.

Once cooked, remove the risoles from the oil and place them on a plate lined with paper towels to drain off excess oil.

Serve the Risoles Sayur hot with sweet chili sauce or your favorite dipping sauce on the side.

Enjoy these delicious Vegetable Spring Rolls as a snack or appetizer!

Feel free to customize the filling with your favorite vegetables or add protein such as shredded chicken or tofu. These Risoles Sayur are best served fresh and crispy, so enjoy them while they're still warm!

Dadar Gulung Pandan (Pandan Rolled Coconut Pancakes)

Ingredients:

For the Pandan Crepes:

- 100 grams all-purpose flour
- 2 eggs
- 200 ml coconut milk
- 100 ml water
- 1 tablespoon pandan extract or 6-8 pandan leaves, blended with water and strained
- Pinch of salt
- Green food coloring (optional)

For the Sweetened Coconut Filling:

- 200 grams grated coconut (fresh or desiccated)
- 100 grams palm sugar or brown sugar
- 1 pandan leaf (optional)
- Pinch of salt

Instructions:

Prepare the Sweetened Coconut Filling:
- In a saucepan, combine the grated coconut, palm sugar, pandan leaf (if using), and a pinch of salt.
- Cook over medium heat, stirring constantly, until the sugar is melted and the mixture is fragrant. This usually takes about 5-7 minutes. Remove from heat and set aside to cool.

Prepare the Pandan Crepes:
- In a mixing bowl, whisk together the all-purpose flour, eggs, coconut milk, water, pandan extract (or pandan juice), and a pinch of salt until smooth. If desired, add a few drops of green food coloring for a brighter green color.
- Strain the batter through a fine sieve to ensure a smooth consistency.

Heat a non-stick pan or crepe pan over medium heat. Lightly grease the pan with oil or butter.

Pour a small ladleful of the pandan crepe batter into the pan, swirling it around to form a thin, even layer.

Cook the crepe for about 1-2 minutes until the edges start to lift and the bottom is lightly golden. Flip the crepe and cook for another 1-2 minutes on the other side.

Remove the cooked crepe from the pan and place it on a plate. Repeat the process with the remaining batter, stacking the crepes on top of each other.

Assemble the Dadar Gulung Pandan:

- Place a spoonful of the sweetened coconut filling along one edge of a pandan crepe.
- Roll up the crepe tightly, enclosing the filling. Repeat with the remaining crepes and filling.

Once all the crepes are filled and rolled, slice the Dadar Gulung Pandan into bite-sized pieces.

Serve the Dadar Gulung Pandan as a delightful snack or dessert.

Enjoy the delicious combination of pandan-infused crepes and sweetened coconut filling!

Feel free to adjust the sweetness of the coconut filling according to your taste preferences. You can also experiment with other fillings such as palm sugar syrup or grated cheese for variety. These Pandan Rolled Coconut Pancakes are best enjoyed fresh, but they can also be stored in an airtight container in the refrigerator for a day or two. Simply reheat gently before serving.

Kue Lumpur Kacang (Peanut Mud Cake)

Ingredients:

- 200 grams roasted peanuts, finely ground
- 200 ml coconut milk
- 150 grams granulated sugar
- 200 grams all-purpose flour
- 1 teaspoon baking powder
- 1/4 teaspoon salt
- Banana leaves or parchment paper, for lining the baking pan

Instructions:

Preheat your oven to 180°C (350°F). Grease a baking dish or cake pan with butter or cooking spray, and line it with banana leaves or parchment paper for easy removal.

In a mixing bowl, combine the finely ground roasted peanuts, coconut milk, and granulated sugar. Mix well until the sugar is dissolved and the mixture is smooth.

In another bowl, sift together the all-purpose flour, baking powder, and salt.

Gradually add the dry ingredients to the peanut mixture, stirring until well combined.

Pour the batter into the prepared baking dish, spreading it out evenly.

Bake in the preheated oven for about 45-60 minutes, or until the top is set and golden brown, and a toothpick inserted into the center comes out clean.

Once baked, remove the Peanut Mud Cake from the oven and let it cool in the pan for about 10-15 minutes.

Once cooled slightly, carefully invert the cake onto a serving plate and remove the banana leaves or parchment paper.

Allow the cake to cool completely before slicing and serving.

Slice the Peanut Mud Cake into squares or rectangles, and serve it as a delicious dessert or snack.

Enjoy the rich and flavorful Peanut Mud Cake with family and friends, savoring its delightful peanut taste!

Store any leftover cake in an airtight container in the refrigerator for up to 3-4 days. You can reheat it in the microwave for a few seconds before serving to enjoy it warm.

Feel free to garnish the Peanut Mud Cake with additional roasted peanuts or a drizzle of chocolate sauce for extra flavor and presentation.

Kue Lumpur Siap (Chicken Mud Cake)

Ingredients:

For the Batter:

- 200 grams all-purpose flour
- 2 eggs
- 200 ml coconut milk
- 100 ml water
- 1 teaspoon ground turmeric
- 1 teaspoon ground coriander
- 1 teaspoon ground cumin
- 1 teaspoon salt
- 1/2 teaspoon ground black pepper
- 2 spring onions, finely chopped
- 2 tablespoons fried shallots (optional)
- Cooking oil, for greasing the pan

For the Chicken Filling:

- 250 grams cooked chicken breast, shredded
- 2 cloves garlic, minced
- 1 small onion, finely chopped
- 1 tablespoon vegetable oil
- Salt and pepper to taste
- Fried shallots for garnish (optional)

Instructions:

Prepare the Chicken Filling:
- Heat vegetable oil in a pan over medium heat. Add minced garlic and chopped onion, and sauté until fragrant.
- Add shredded chicken breast to the pan and stir-fry until heated through. Season with salt and pepper to taste. Remove from heat and set aside.

Prepare the Batter:

- In a mixing bowl, whisk together all-purpose flour, eggs, coconut milk, water, ground turmeric, ground coriander, ground cumin, salt, and ground black pepper until smooth.
- Stir in finely chopped spring onions and fried shallots (if using).

Assemble the Kue Lumpur Siap:
- Grease a heatproof dish or pan with cooking oil. Pour a thin layer of the batter into the dish, spreading it evenly.
- Spread the cooked chicken filling evenly over the batter layer.
- Pour the remaining batter over the chicken filling, covering it completely.

Cook the Kue Lumpur Siap:
- Steam the dish or pan over high heat for about 30-40 minutes, or until the batter is firm and cooked through.
- Once cooked, remove the Kue Lumpur Siap from the steamer and let it cool slightly.

Serve:
- Cut the Kue Lumpur Siap into squares or diamond shapes.
- Garnish with fried shallots (if desired) and serve warm as a savory snack or appetizer.

Enjoy the unique and flavorful Kue Lumpur Siap with its savory chicken filling and spiced batter!

Bika Ambon (Indonesian Honeycomb Cake)

Ingredients:

- 250 grams tapioca flour
- 100 grams rice flour
- 200 grams granulated sugar
- 5 eggs
- 200 ml coconut milk
- 100 ml water
- 1/2 teaspoon active dry yeast
- 1/2 teaspoon baking powder
- 1/4 teaspoon salt
- 2 pandan leaves, knotted (optional, for flavor)
- Green food coloring (optional)
- Oil or margarine, for greasing the pan

Instructions:

In a small bowl, mix the active dry yeast with 1 tablespoon of warm water and a pinch of sugar. Set it aside for about 5-10 minutes until it becomes frothy.
In a large mixing bowl, whisk together the tapioca flour, rice flour, granulated sugar, and salt until well combined.
In a separate bowl, beat the eggs until light and frothy.
Gradually add the beaten eggs to the flour mixture, stirring continuously to prevent lumps.
In a saucepan, heat the coconut milk, water, and pandan leaves over low heat until warm. Remove from heat and let it cool slightly.
Gradually add the warm coconut milk mixture to the batter, stirring until smooth and well combined. Add the activated yeast mixture and stir to incorporate.
Cover the batter with a clean kitchen towel and let it rest in a warm place for about 1-2 hours, or until it becomes bubbly and slightly risen.
After the batter has fermented, remove the pandan leaves and discard them. Stir in the baking powder and green food coloring (if using) until evenly distributed.
Preheat your oven to 180°C (350°F). Grease a round cake pan with oil or margarine and line the bottom with parchment paper.
Pour the batter into the prepared cake pan, filling it about 3/4 full.

Bake in the preheated oven for about 40-50 minutes, or until the top is golden brown and a toothpick inserted into the center comes out clean.

Once baked, remove the Bika Ambon from the oven and let it cool in the pan for about 10-15 minutes.

Carefully transfer the cake to a wire rack to cool completely.

Once cooled, slice the Bika Ambon into pieces and serve.

Enjoy the delightful Bika Ambon with its unique texture and sweet flavor as a snack or dessert!